A MIDDLE EAST STUDIES HANDBOOK

A MIDDLE EAST STUDIES
HANDBOOK

JERE L. BACHARACH

UNIVERSITY OF WASHINGTON PRESS
Seattle • London

A Middle East Studies Handbook is a revised and expanded
version of A Near East Studies Handbook (copyright © 1974,
1976 by the University of Washington Press).

Library of Congress Cataloging-in-Publication Data

Bacharach, Jere L., 1938-
    A Middle East studies handbook.

    Rev. Ed. of: A Near East studies handbook. Rev. ed.
c1976.
    Includes bibliographical references and index.
    1. Islamic Empire--History--Handbooks, manuals, etc.
2. Near East--History--1517-   --Handbooks, manuals,
etc. I. Bacharach, Jere L., 1938-   . Near East
studies handbook. II. Title
DS61.B3 1984   956   84-2225
ISBN 0-295-96144-9 (pbk.)

TO

Ruth • *Debby* • *Julie*

Contents

Preface

Increasing interest in the Middle East, particularly over the last decade, necessitated a major revision and updating of the volume, originally published in 1974 entitled *A Near East Studies Handbook: 570-1974*. The new title reflects the growing use of the term "Middle East." The geographical area covered includes Iran, Turkey, Egypt, the Fertile Crescent (modern Iraq, Syria, Lebanon, Jordan and Israel), and the Arabian Peninsula. Occasionally material touching on Libya, the Sudan, the Ottomans in Europe, the Muslims in Spain or Afghanistan has been added. A more accurate (though less popular) geographic description of this area would be, simply, Southwest Asia and Egypt. And this is used on most of the historical maps in Chapter VIII. The work spans the centuries from the birth of Muhammad the Prophet — traditionally 570 C.E. to the events of autumn, 1983.

As there is no single, accepted transliteration system from the Arabic script to the Latin alphabet, the first chapter identifies some of the common Latin variations for Arabic consonant and vowel sounds. A complete transliteration table, as used by the Middle East Studies Association, is provided. A new addition to this chapter is a section on Islamic names.

The second chapter is a list of the abbreviations for 89 periodicals and reference works, which represents a 20-percent increase over previous editions. The third chapter includes a brief discussion on the problems of converting dates from the Muslim to the Western calendar (and vice versa), a new section on Muslim holidays, and a date conversion table from 622 C.E. to 2000 C.E.

The fourth chapter involves the combining of three chapters from the earlier editions. All of the material related to lists of dynasties, rulers, administrators and, when appropriate, a genealogy table, has been consolidated in this chapter. The material is now easier to locate, but has the added advantage of placing related data together. Chapter V is comprised of six supplementary charts illustrating language families, tribal ties and *ṣūfī isnād*s.

The Chronology is now Chapter VI and covers

events into December, 1983. In addition to including the post-1976 material, the data in the earlier editions have been strengthened. The result has been a 25-percent increase in the number of items. Chapter VII lists 80 twentieth-century social, political and economic organizations by their acronyms — an increase of almost 20 percent.

There are now 51 maps in Chapter VIII, the Historical Atlas. This atlas now includes city maps of Jerusalem, Istanbul, Beirut, and major developments in the Middle East since 1976. As an aid to those interested in contemporary affairs, six maps with only the major cities indicated have been added to this section. The atlas is thoroughly indexed with its own index. Chapter IX, a Gazetteer, is an entirely new feature of this edition. It lists alphabetically approximately 125 cities with alternate spellings, population figures, and longitudes and latitudes. Chapter X is a Glossary of 300 items, an increase of almost 25 percent over earlier editions.

Besides my debt to scholarly works which I acknowledge in almost every chapter, a number of individuals have aided me and I wish to thank them, recognizing that others could have been added to this list:

Barb Shurin typed this entire manuscript and designed it. George Shurin patiently persevered through all the hours Barb and I spent working on this book. Alice Alden, as always, demonstrated her professional skills in preparing the maps and genealogy tables. April Richardson did additional design work. Felicia J. Hecker offered valuable, last-minute suggestions. The University of Washington Press suggested the idea for a revision and was very supportive during the long process of preparing the manuscript. Additional financial support from Exxon Corporation was greatly appreciated.

Many scholars provided information and ideas to improve this edition of the handbook. In particular, I wish to thank the contributions and comments of Michael Bates, Jacob Goldberg, Arthur Goldschmidt, Jacob Landau, Christopher Murphy, Tamara Sonn, Charles Woods, Khalid Yahya, and Mohsen Zakari. The names of those who helped in the previous editions — Calvin Allen, Andrew S.

Ehrenkreutz, Nicholas Heer, Judith S. Heide, Michael M. Pixley, Stephanie Sayers, Walid Shahouk, and Farhat J. Ziadeh — should not be forgotten. Professor Janet Abu Lughod generously gave me permission to adapt her map of al-Fusṭāṭ (Cairo), and I wish to thank her.

Finally, Ruth, Debby and Julie were very patient and supportive as I reworked the manuscript while trying to juggle a dozen other activities, and I am very pleased to dedicate this work to them. Obviously, any errors remain my responsibility.

A number of the maps were adapted from previously produced works:

* From *An Atlas of Middle Eastern Affairs*, by Robert C. Kingsbury and Norman J.G. Pounds (New York: Frederick A. Praeger, Inc., 1963). Excerpted and adapted by permission.

* From *History of the Arabs*, by Philip Hitti (New York: St. Martin's Press, 1965). Excerpted and adapted by permission.

* From *The Historical Atlas of the Muslim Peoples*, by R. Roolvink (Amsterdam: Djambatan, Inc., 1957). Excerpted and adapted by permission.

* From *South West Asia*, by William C. Brice (London: University of London Press, Ltd., 1967). Excerpted and adapted by permission.

* From "La Répartition Confessionelle au Liban et l'Équilibre de l'État Libanais," by Etienne de Vaumas, *Revue de Géographie Alpine* 43 (1965). Excerpted and adapted by permission.

* From *The Historical Atlas of Jerusalem: A Brief Illustrated Survey*, by Dan Bahat (New York: Charles Scribner's Sons, 1973). Excerpted and adapted by permission.

A number of changes have been made for this reprint thanks to the valuable suggestions of Arthur Goldschmidt and Gustav Bayerle.

A MIDDLE EAST STUDIES HANDBOOK

I. Transliteration Systems and Islamic Names

Transliteration Systems

Because there is no single, universally accepted system of transliteration from the Arabic script to the Latin alphabet, one often finds variant spellings of words that can confuse the unwary. As an example, for the Holy Book of the Muslims (or Moslems), one will see "Qur'ān" or "Koran."

The following remarks indicate some of the problems one may face when coming across Arabic, Persian and Ottoman words written in a Western script. The section includes the transliteration system used by the Middle East Studies Association, as well as a number of other important variants. A very good discussion of many of the problems is in Marshall G.S. Hodgson, *The Venture of Islam*, 3 vols. (Chicago: University of Chicago Press, 1974), 1:8-20.

For words transliterated from Arabic, the major variants are q or k, j or dj, u or o, i or y, or e. In the preceding example, there was "Qur'ān" or "Koran," illustrating two variants. The *Encyclopedia of Islam*, in the manner of the old European system, used "k" and "dj" for "q" and "j," respectively. Therefore, the modern Muslim reformist, Jamāl al-Dīn al-Afghānī, is found in the *Encyclopedia of Islam* under "dj." Another problem is the use of the definite article "al." It can be transliterated according to its spelling, which always includes the "l," or according to its pronunciation. In the latter case, the "l" is assimilated when followed by

certain letters — t, th, d, dh, r, z, s, sh, ṣ, ḍ, ṭ, ẓ and n — e.g.: *al-dīn* or *ad-dīn*.

The transliteration system used for Persian has been heavily influenced by the forms used for Arabic. As a whole, this has not caused serious problems, except in the transliteration of vowels and a few consonants (e.g.: i or e, u or o, w or v, and various forms for diphthongs). One may, therefore, find Isfahan or Esfahan, Mulk or Molk, Firdawsi or Ferdosi, and Qazwin or Qazvin.

Ottoman Turkish is the most troublesome, and even the Library of Congress has not adopted an official transliteration system. The fullest discussion can be found in an article by Eleazar Birnbaum, "The Transliteration of Ottoman Turkish for Library and General Purposes," *Journal of the American Oriental Society*, (1967) 87:122-156, where he suggests his own system. The modern Turks, having adopted a Latin script in 1928, have their own system of transliterating Ottoman. Therefore, if one were to take the Ottoman word for "member of the old Turkish dynasty": عثمانلى, it could be transliterated as ꜤUthmānlī, ꜤOsmānlī or Osmanlı, using an Arabic-based system, MESA rules and modern Turkish forms, respectively.

Finally, a graphic but special example of transliteration: the Persian word for "teacher" or "educated person" is خواجه ; and it can be found as *hoca* in modern Turkish, but it will be found in the *Encyclopedia of Islam* under *kh^w ādja*!

	MESA System (1983)			Selected Variations		
Arabic	Persian	Ottoman Turkish	Modern Turkish	Encyclopedia of Islam	Geschichte des arabischen Schrifttums	Encyclopaedia Iranica
ا '	'	'	--			
ب b	b	b	b or p			
پ --	p	p	p			
ت t	t	t	t			
ث th	s	s	s	th	t	t, s
ج j	j	c	c	dj	ǧ	ǰ
چ --	ch	ç	ç	č		č
ح ḥ	ḥ	ḥ	h			
خ kh	kh	h	h	kh	ḥ	
د d	d	d	d			
ذ dh	z	z	z	dh	d	d, z
ر r	r	r	r			
ز z	z	z	z			
ژ --	zh	j	j	zh		zh
س s	s	s	s			
ش sh	sh	ş	ş	sh	š	š
ص ṣ	ṣ	ṣ	s			
ض ḍ	ż	ż	z			
ط ṭ	ṭ	ṭ	t			
ظ ẓ	ẓ	ẓ	z			
ع c	c	c	--	c		
غ gh	gh	g or ğ	g or ğ	gh	ġ	ḡ
ف f	f	f	f			
ق q	q	ḳ	k	ḳ		
ك k	k or g	k,ñ,y,ğ	k,n,y,ğ	g		
گ --	g	g	g			
ل l	l	l	l			
م m	m	m	m			
ن n	n	n	n			
ه h	h	h*	h*			
و w	v or u	v	v	ou		v, w

[continued]

| Arabic | MESA System (1983) | | | Selected Variations | | |
	Persian	Ottoman Turkish	Modern Turkish	Encyclopedia of Islam	Geschichte des arabischen Schrifttums	Encyclopaedia Iranica
ى y	y	y	y			
ة -a**						
ال al-***						
ٔل 'l-***						

* When not final.
** -at when in construct state.
*** The "l" in the article may change to t, th, d, dh, r, z, s, sh, ṣ, ḍ, ṭ, ẓ or n
    if the word to which it is attached begins with that letter; e.ġ., al-dīn or ad-dīn.

V O W E L S

Arabic and Persian	Ottoman Turkish	Modern Turkish
Long: ا or â ى	â words of Arabic	â
û و	û and Persian	û
î ي	î origin only	î
Doubled: iyy (final form î) ـيّ	iy (final form: î)	iy (final form: î)
uww (final form û), etc. وّ	uvv	uvv
Diphthongs: au or aw و	ev or av[+]	ev or av[+]
ai or ay ـى	ey or ay[+]	ey or ay[+]
Short: a ´	a or e	a or e
u '	u or ü	u or ü
	o or ö	o or ö
i ِ	ı or i	ı or i

+ Not MESA system.

Islamic Names

Not only does the problem of transliterating Islamic names pose difficulties; e.g., ᶜAbd al-Nāṣir vs. Nasser and al-Qadhdhāfī vs. Qaddafi, but identifying which part of the name to use — particularly a pre-19th-century one — is not always clear. Traditional Middle Eastern names are composed of a number of elements, beginning with the name given at birth (*ism*) and the name of the father (*nasab*). The individual may become a parent or acquire an epithet or honorific sense of parentage (*kunya*). It is also very common for a person in power to acquire an honorific title (*laqab*); while everyone would acquire titles reflecting their occupations, places of origins, etc. (*nisbah*).

In medieval dictionaries and in the British Museum, most Muslims are listed by their *ism* or proper name. An *ism* can be:

- a Qur'ānic form of a Biblical name; e.g., Sulaymān (Solomon) or Hārūn (Aaron);

- a purely Arabic name; e.g., Aḥmad, ᶜAlī, Ḥusayn or Muḥammad;

- a compound name associated with God, implying "servant" of God; e.g., ᶜAbd Allāh or Abdullah, ᶜAbd al-Malik. The "ᶜAbd" may not be dropped as it is part of the name; or

- a non-Arabic name; e.g., Rustam, Hulagu or Timur.

The *nasab* refers to one's pedigree or ancestors and is *ibn* (son of) or *bint* (daughter of) plus an *ism*. Sometimes the *nasab* becomes the common name for a family and does not reflect an actual parent/child relationship. The famous 14th-century historian-thinker, Ibn Khaldūn, is not the son of Khaldūn, who was a more distant relative. In Persian an "i" is added to indicate the *nasab* in names, or "zāde" is used as a suffix to the father's name or title. Turkish uses "oghlu" or "zāde" as a suffix to indicate the *nasab*. The *kunya* is the term *abū* (father) and, occasionally, *umm* (mother), followed by the real name of a child or an attribute; e.g., Abū al-Faḍl is either "the father of al-Faḍl" or "the father of merit."

The *laqab* is an honorific title or descriptive epithet which can be earned or acquired as an attribute or nickname. Many *laqab*s are compound names which end in *al-dīn* (religion), *al-dawla* (state) and *al-mulk* (kingdom), and were originally held by powerful political and military figures, but then became more common. Some examples are:

- Jalāl al-Dīn [Majesty of the Faith],

- Nāṣir al-Dawla [Defender of the State], and

- Niẓām al-Mulk [Order of the Kingdom].

Other *laqab*s could be nicknames; e.g., al-Aṭrash (the Deaf); or honorific titles for ᶜAbbāsid caliphs; e.g., al-Rashīd (the Rightly Guided).

The *nisbah* constitutes the broadest category and can include profession, place or origin, birth or residence. Individuals can have more than one *nisbah*, and they usually begin with the article "al-" and end with a long "i." Thus, an individual can have *nisbah*s, such as:

- al-Qudsī [from Jerusalem],

- al-Juhaynī [of the Juhayn tribe],

- al-Ṣayrafī [the money-changer].

The full name of the famous 15th-century scholar, known as al-Suyūṭī (or Jalāl al-Dīn al-Suyūṭī), was ᶜAbd al-Raḥmān b. [Ibn] Abī Bakr b. Muḥammad b. Khidr b. Ayyūb b. Muḥammad b. al-Humān al-Khuḍayrī al-Suyūṭī. Looking up the full name in a source could pose many problems. The easiest way to locate information on pre-Modern figures is to check the *Encyclopedia of Islam* (*EI*), either edition, under the name by which the individual is best known; e.g.: al-Suyūṭī.

For a more detailed discussion of Muslim names, see:

- C.H. Phillips, ed., *Handbook of Oriental History* (London: Royal Historical Society, 1951), pp. 7-9;

- Marshall G.S. Hodgson, *The Venture of Islam*, 3 vols. (Chicago: University of Chicago Press, 1974), 1:16-20.

II. Periodicals and Reference Works

An extensive list of periodical abbreviations can be found in James D. Pearson, *Index Islamicus, 1906-1955* (Cambridge: Heffer, 1953), and the succeeding supplements. Another excellent source, particularly for journals concerned with the contemporary Middle East, is the last annual issue (No. 4) of each year of the *Middle East Journal*, where an extensive list of sources with abbreviations is cited.

Annotated bibliographies for Middle East studies are limited. For the Medieval period — that is, until the rise and success of the Ottomans — the best annotated bibliography is Jean Sauvaget, *Introduction to the History of the Muslim East: A Bibliographical Guide*, edited/revised by Claude Cahen (Berkeley: University of California Press, 1965). Another valuable tool, but with fewer annotations, is Derek Hopwood and Diana Grimwood-Jones, *Middle East and Islam: A Bibliographical Introduction* (Zurich: Inter-Documentation Company, 1972). A work which is very useful for many libraries for the Medieval and Modern Eras is David W. Littlefield, *The Islamic Near East and North Africa: An Annotated Guide for Public and College Libraries and Readers* (Littleton Co., Libraries Unlimited, 1977).

For the more Modern Era, there are a number of references which one may use:

* *The Arab Culture and Society in Change: A Partially Annotated Bibliography* (Beirut: St. Joseph's University, 1973) has almost 5,000 items.

* George Atiyeh, *The Contemporary Middle East, 1948-1973: A Selective Annotated Bibliography* (Boston: G.K. Hall, 1975), is also very useful.

* Another source is Henry Field, *Bibliography of Southwestern Asia* (Coral Gables, FL: University of Miami Press, 1953-), vol. 1-.

For those seeking periodical material on topics related to the Middle East, there are two major sources for material published in the West. *Index Islamicus*, cited above, has extensive lists of articles on pre-Modern topics. It is now pub-lished quarterly and, every five years, gathered into a single volume. The fifth supplementary volume has just been published in two segments: one for articles and one for books. *Mideast File* (Medford, NJ: Learned Information) is a quarterly begun in March 1982 by the Shiloah Center for Middle Eastern and African Studies, Tel Aviv, Israel. It has annotations on books and articles published in Arabic, English, French, German, Hebrew, Persian and Turkish. It emphasizes the contemporary world and the social sciences. Each issue of *MEJ* has an extensive list of recent articles arranged by topic. These periodical lists were gathered together in Peter M. Rossi and Wayne E. White, *Articles on the Middle East, 1947-1971: A Cumulation of the Bibliographies from the MIDDLE EAST JOURNAL* (Ann Arbor: Pierian Press, 1980). For publications in Arabic, there is *Al-Fihrist: Kashf al-Dawriyyāt al-ᶜArabiyyah* (Beirut: Watwat al-Zarif, 1982), which appears quarterly and has subject headings and cross-listings.

For those seeking book reviews of works related to Middle East topics, the following tools may be helpful: Wolfgang H. Behn, *Islamic Book Review Index* (Berlin: Behn, 1982), has an extensive coverage of European language reviews. Volume I lists approximately 2,600 titles. At the end of each issue of *MEJ* there is a list of the books reviewed in the journals which are surveyed by *MEJ*. There is no cumulative index of all of these references.

Standard references for most book reviews are:

* *The Combined Retrospective Index to Book Reviews in Scholarly Journals: 1886-1974* (New York: Research Publications, Inc., 1982).

* *The Book Review Index: 1969-1979, 1980-*, which is published bi-monthly, and then consolidated annually.

* *An Index to Book Reviews, 1960-*.

* *Current Book Review Citations, 1976-*, which is published monthly, except February and August, and is then consolidated annually.

List of Abbreviations

AARP	*Art and Archeology Research Papers*		GMS	*Gibb Memorial Series*
AAS	*Asian and African Studies*		HO	Spuler, B. (Ed.). *Handbuch der Orientalistik* (Leiden, 1952-)
AHR	*American Historical Review*			
AHS	*African Historical Studies*			
AI	*Ars Islamica*		IA	*İslam Ansiklopedisi*
AIYS News.	*American Institute for Yemen Studies Newsletter*		IC	*Islamic Culture*
			IEJ	*Israel Exploration Journal*
And.	*al-Andalus*		IJAHS	*International Journal of African Historical Studies*
AO	*Acta orientalia*		IJMES	*International Journal of Middle East Studies*
ARCE News.	*American Research Center in Egypt Newsletter*		IJTS	*International Journal of Turkish Studies*
ArO	*Archiv orientální*		IQ	*Islamic Quarterly*
ArOtt	*Archivum Ottomanicum*		IrS	*Iranian Studies*
			IS	*Islamic Studies*
BEO	*Bulletin d'études orientales*			
BGA	*Bibliotheca geographorum Arabicorum*		JA	*Journal asiatique*
BIE	*Bulletin de l'Institut d'Égypte*		JAH	*Journal of African History*
BIFAO	*Bulletin de l'Institut Français d'Archéologie Orientale*		JAL	*Journal of Arab Literature*
BRISMES Bull.	*British Society for Middle East Studies Bulletin*		JAOS	*Journal of the American Oriental Society*
BSOAS	*Bulletin of the School of Oriental & African Studies* (London University)		JCH	*Journal of Contemporary History*
			JESHO	*Journal of the Economic and Social History of the Orient*
BZ	*Byzantinische Zeitschrift*		JJS	*Journal of Jewish Studies*
			JMAS	*Journal of Modern African Studies*
CH	*Current History*		JMH	*Journal of Modern History*
CIA	*Corpus Inscriptionum Arabicorum*		JNES	*Journal of Near Eastern Studies*
CSSH	*Comparative Studies in Society and History*		JPS	*Journal of Palestine Studies*
			JQ	*The Jerusalem Quarterly*
DI	*Der Islam*		JRAS	*Journal of the Royal Asiatic Society of Great Britain and Ireland*
EHR	*English Historical Review/Economic Historical Review*		JSAI	*Jerusalem Studies in Arabic and Islam*
EI¹	*The Encyclopaedia of Islam.* 4 Vols., Supp. (Leiden, 1913-1942)		JSS	*Journal of Semitic Studies*
EI²	*The Encyclopaedia of Islam.* 2nd ed. (Leiden, 1954-)		JWH	*Journal of World History*
EIr	*Encyclopaedia Iranica*		MEED	*Middle East Economic Digest*
			MEF	*Middle East Forum*
GAL	Brockelmann, C. *Geschichte der arabischen Litteratur.* 2nd ed., 2 Vols. (Leiden, 1943-1949)		MEJ	*Middle East Journal*
			MELA Notes	*Middle East Librarians' Association Notes*
GALS	Brockelmann, C. *Geschichte der arabischen Litteratur Supplement.* 3 Vols. (Leiden, 1937-1942)		MEOC News.	*Middle East Outreach Coordinators' Newsletter*
GAS	Sezgin, F. *Geschichte des arabischen Schrifttums* (Leiden, 1967-)		MERIP Reports	*Middle East Research and Information Project Reports*

MES	*Middle Eastern Studies*	RHC	*Recueil des historiens des croisades*
MESA Bull.	*Middle East Studies Association Bulletin*	RIMA	*Revue de l'Institut des Manuscripts Arabes*
MIDEO	*Mélanges des l'Institut Dominicain d'Études Orientales du Caire*	RMM	*Revue de monde musulman*
MIFAO	*Mémoires de l'Institut Français d'Archéologie Orientale*	ROC	*Revue de l'Orient chrétien*
MSG News.	*Maghrib Studies Group Newsletter*	RSO	*Rivista degli studi orientali*
MW	*Muslim World* [formerly *Moslem World*]	SEI	*Shorter Encyclopaedia of Islam*
		SI	*Studia Islamica*
NAHIA News.	*National Association of Historians of Islamic Art Newsletter*	SIS News.	*Society for Iranian Studies Newsletter*
		Spec.	*Speculum*
OM	*Oriente moderno*		
Ors	*Oriens*	TSA Bull.	*Turkish Studies Association Bulletin*
PO	*Patrologia Orientalis*	WI	*Die Welt des Islams*
		WO	*Die Welt des Orients*
RAAD	*Revue de l'Académie Arabe de Damas*		
REI	*Revue des études islamiques*	ZDMG	*Zeitschrift der Deutschen Morgenländischen Gesellschaft*
REJ	*Revue des études juives*		
RH	*Revue historique*		

III. Islamic Calendar and Conversion Table

Caliph ^{c}Umār established the first year of the Muslim calendar as the year in which Muḥammad left Mecca for Medina. This departure or *hijra* became the name for the Islamic calendar (A.H. = *Anno Hejirae*) and 1/1/1 *hijra* was calculated as 16 July 622. The Islamic calendar, like many other calendars, is based on a lunar year of approximately 354 days, or about 11 days less than a solar year. In order to keep the lunar months in alignment with the major seasons, most users of a lunar calendar interpolate an extra or 13th month.

The Muslim calendar has no extra month, as a Qur'ānic revelation (Sūra IX, Verse 30) fixed the calendar year at 12 lunar months. The net result is that knowing the Muslim month and year in which an event took place does not indicate the corresponding season or specific month in the Gregorian (Western) solar calendar. One relatively easy way to calculate the Muslim equivalent for a Western date, and vice versa, is to use the formulae which follow:

$$H = 1.013 \ [W - 622]$$
$$W = H - H/31 + 622$$

Another procedure is to use the accompanying Conversion Table where Muslim dates are listed and the equivalent Western date can be found to the right of them.

A few words of caution are necessary before using any table to calculate the exact Western date for a given Islamic-era date (or vice versa). The Islamic calendar is based upon observation of the moon, not a fixed number of days. Therefore, although the tables and officially printed calendars say a new Islamic-era month begins on a particular Western day, unless the ^{c}*ulamā'* see the new moon, the month has not begun. This tradition persists today when the ^{c}*ulamā'*, and not the government calendar, determine when the Muslim month of fasting (Ramaḍān) begins and ends. The net result is that a local calendar can be up to two days different from the calculated tables.

A second problem is that an Islamic calendar month does not have to start on the same Western calendar day in two different cities. For example, the first day of Ramaḍān 500 A.H. in Cairo may or may not be the same day of the week in Baghdad, or any other city.

Finally, the Muslim day begins at sunset. Therefore, when calculating the corresponding Western date for an event held in the evening on the Islamic calendar, it is necessary to subtract one day from the calculated Western date. All of the preceding is a warning not to push an argument on the relationship between two very close pre-1800 events if it is based primarily on their respective Islamic (or corresponding Western) dates — unless those dates have been very carefully checked.

If you have a Muslim date with a month and wish to calculate the approximate Western date using the accompanying table, the following procedure should be used: first, locate on the table the Western date for the first day of that particular Muslim year. Then add the appropriate number of months of the Muslim date to the Western date, and that will create a ballpark estimate. The Muslim months are as follows:

Muharram	Jumādā l-ūlā	Ramaḍān
Safar	Jumādā l-ākhira	Shawwāl
Rabī^c al-awwal	Rajab	Dhū-l-Qa^{c}da
Rabī^c al-thānī	Sha^{c}bān	Dhū-l-Ḥijja

Marshall G.S. Hodgson, *The Venture of Islam*, 3 vols. (Chicago: University of Chicago Press, 1974), 1:22, lists the most common month names of the solar calendar. They are repeated here in both their Arabic and Persian forms:

Arabic		Persian	
Kānūn al-thānī	Jan.	Bahman	Jan./Feb.
Shubāṭ	Feb.	Isfand	Feb./March
Adhār	March	Farvardīn	Mar./April
Nīsān	April	Urdī-bihisht	April/May
Ayyār	May	Khurdād	May/June
Ḥazīrān	June	Tīr	June/July
Tamūz	July	Murdād	July/Aug.
Āb	Aug.	Shahrīvar	
Aylūl	Sept.	[Shahrīr]	Aug./Sept.
Tishrīn al-awwal	Oct.	Mihr	Sept./Oct.
Tishrīn al-thānī	Nov.	Ābān	Oct./Nov.
Kānūn al-awwal	Dec.	Āzar	Nov./Dec.
		Day	Dec./Jan.

In order to calculate the exact Western day

for a Muslim day, more elaborate tables than the one in this handbook must be used. The work by G.S.P. Freeman-Grenville, *The Muslim and Christian Calendars* (London: Oxford University Press, 1963), has clear instructions and can be used for such purposes. A more detailed work which includes other calendars, including the special Ottoman financial calendar, is E. Mahler, *Wustenfeld-Mahlersche Vergleichungs-Tabellen der mohammedanischen und christlichen Zeitrechnung* (Leipzig, 1926; 3rd ed., Wiesbaden, 1961).

The best source for transforming the various calendars used by the Ottomans into Gregorian dates is Faik Resit Unat, *Hicri Tarihleri Milade Tarihe Cevirme Kilavuzu*, 3rd ed. (Ankara, Turkey: Turk Tarih kurumu basimlvi, 1959).

A general survey of the types of calendars found in the Islamic world is H. Taqizadeh, "Various Eras and Calendars Used in the Countries of Islam," *BSOAS*, vol. 9 (1937-1939):902-999; and vol. 10 (1940-1942):107-132. The most comprehensive list of tables of the numerous pre-Ottoman medieval calendars is found in V. Grummel, *La chronologie (Traite d'études byzantines)*, vol. 1, ed. P. Lemerle (Paris, 1958). Among the calendars found in this work are Julian, Armenian, Coptic, Sassanian, Mongolian and Muslim calendars, plus data on comets, eclipses, earthquakes, etc. to 1453.

Selected Muslim Holidays

• Muharram 1 [*Ras al-Sana*: The New Year] is the first day of the first month and, while it is not a particularly religious holiday, it now is celebrated throughout the Islamic world.

• Muharram 10 [*^{C}Ashura'*: The Tenth] is the day on which many pious Muslims fast from dawn to sunset. For Shi^{C}i Muslims this day is of particular importance, as it commemorates the assassination of ^{C}Ali's son, Husayn.

• Rabi^C al-awwal 12 [*Mawlid al-Nabi*; The Prophet's Birthday] is a holiday associated with festivities and exchanging of gifts. Often passages eulogizing Muhammad are read.

• Rajab 27 [*Lailat al-Isra' wa'l-mi^{C}raj*: The Night of Journey and Ascent] commemorates Muhammad's night journey from Mecca to the Haram al-Sharif area in Jerusalem and his ascent to Heaven

and return to Jerusalem, and then Mecca — all in one night. This night is traditionally celebrated by prayers.

• Sha^{C}ban 14 [*Lailat al-Bara'a*: Night of Remembrance] is, according to Muslim tradition, the night God approaches earth to grant forgiveness for an individual's sins.

• Ramadan [ninth month of the Muslim year] is devoted to spiritual purification through the abstinence from food, drink and physical pleasure from dawn until dusk.

• Ramadan 27 [*Lailat al-Qadar*: Night of Power and Greatness] is considered a particularly holy time, as it is the night, by tradition, on which Muhammad received the first revelation.

• Shawwal 1 [*^{C}id al-Fitr*: The Lesser Feast] is the most joyous festival in the Islamic calendar and marks the end of abstinence during Ramadan.

• Dhu-1-Hijja 1-10: The period in which Muslims are to undertake a pilgrimage to Mecca and its environs in imitation of Muhammad's last pilgrimage.

• Dhu-1-Hijja 10 [*^{C}id al-Adha*: The Greater Feast] is the high point of the pilgrimage and is celebrated by Muslims throughout the world, even if not actually participating in the pilgrimage. It is most often marked by the slaughtering of lambs and the distribution of meat to the needy.

Hebrew Calendar

Jews, for religious purposes and within their own communities, use a lunar calendar composed of 12 lunar months. In order to keep fall and spring holidays in the appropriate season, a 13th month — called the Second Adar — is added after the sixth Jewish month [Adar] in the following 19-year cycle: 3rd year, 6th, 8th, 11th, 14th, 17th and 19th year. Thus, a particular holiday may vary by 20 days between years, but it will always be in the same season.

The Jewish New Year is in the fall, usually in September. In order to calculate the Western year since the rise of Islam in which most of the Jewish year falls, add 240 to the Hebrew date, and then subtract 4,000.

Calendar Conversion Table

Hijra Year	Western Date of Muḥarram 1	Hijra Year	Western Date of Muḥarram 1	Hijra Year	Western Date of Muḥarram 1	Hijra Year	Western Date of Muḥarram 1
1	16 July 622	65	18 Aug 684	128	3 Oct 745	191	17 Nov 806
2	5 July 623	66	8 Aug 685	129	22 Sept 746	192	6 Nov 807
3	24 June 624	67	28 July 686	130	11 Sept 747	193	25 Oct 808
4	13 June 625	68	18 July 687	131	31 Aug 748	194	15 Oct 809
5	2 June 626	69	6 July 688	132	20 Aug 749	195	4 Oct 810
6	23 May 627	70	25 June 689	133	9 Aug 750	196	23 Sept 811
7	11 May 628	71	15 June 690	134	30 July 751	197	12 Sept 812
8	1 May 629	72	4 June 691	135	18 July 752	198	1 Sept 813
9	20 Apr 630	73	23 May 692	136	7 July 753	199	22 Aug 814
10	9 Apr 631	74	13 May 693	137	27 June 754	200	11 Aug 815
11	29 Mar 632	75	2 May 694	138	16 June 755	201	30 July 816
12	18 Mar 633	76	21 Apr 695	139	5 June 756	202	20 July 817
13	7 Mar 634	77	10 Apr 696	140	25 May 757	203	9 July 818
14	25 Feb 635	78	30 Mar 697	141	14 May 758	204	28 June 819
15	14 Feb 636	79	20 Mar 698	142	4 May 759	205	17 June 820
16	2 Feb 637	80	9 Mar 699	143	22 Apr 760	206	6 June 821
17	23 Jan 638			144	11 Apr 761	207	27 May 822
18	12 Jan 639	81	26 Feb 700	145	1 Apr 762	208	16 May 823
19	2 Jan 640	82	15 Feb 701	146	21 Mar 763	209	4 May 824
20	21 Dec 640	83	4 Feb 702	147	10 Mar 764	210	24 Apr 825
21	10 Dec 641	84	24 Jan 703	148	27 Feb 765	211	13 Apr 826
22	30 Nov 642	85	14 Jan 704	149	16 Feb 766	212	2 Apr 827
23	19 Nov 643	86	2 Jan 705	150	6 Feb 767	213	22 Mar 828
24	7 Nov 644	87	23 Dec 705	151	26 Jan 768	214	11 Mar 829
25	28 Oct 645	88	12 Dec 706	152	14 Jan 769	215	25 Feb 830
26	17 Oct 646	89	1 Dec 707	153	4 Jan 770	216	18 Feb 831
27	7 Oct 647	90	20 Nov 708	154	24 Dec 770	217	7 Feb 832
28	25 Sept 648	91	9 Nov 709	155	13 Dec 771	218	27 Jan 833
29	14 Sept 649	92	29 Oct 710	156	2 Dec 772	219	16 Jan 834
30	4 Sept 650	93	19 Oct 711	157	21 Nov 773	220	5 Jan 835
31	24 Aug 651	94	7 Oct 712	158	11 Nov 774	221	26 Dec 835
32	12 Aug 652	95	26 Sept 713	159	31 Oct 775	222	14 Dec 836
33	2 Aug 653	96	16 Sept 714	160	19 Oct 776	223	3 Dec 837
34	22 July 654	97	5 Sept 715	161	9 Oct 777	224	23 Nov 838
35	11 July 655	98	25 Aug 716	162	28 Sept 778	225	12 Nov 839
36	30 June 656	99	14 Aug 717	163	17 Sept 779	226	31 Oct 840
37	19 June 657	100	3 Aug 718	164	6 Sept 780	227	21 Oct 841
38	9 June 658	101	24 July 719	165	26 Aug 781	228	10 Oct 842
39	29 May 659	102	12 July 720	166	15 Aug 782	229	20 Sept 843
40	17 May 660	103	1 July 721	167	5 Aug 783	230	18 Sept 844
41	7 May 661	104	21 June 722	168	24 July 784	231	7 Sept 845
42	26 Apr 662	105	10 June 723	169	14 July 785	232	28 Aug 846
43	15 Apr 663	106	29 May 724	170	3 July 786	233	17 Aug 847
44	4 Apr 664	107	19 May 725	171	22 June 787	234	5 Aug 848
45	24 Mar 665	108	8 May 726	172	11 June 788	235	26 July 849
46	13 Mar 666	109	28 Apr 727	173	31 May 789	236	15 July 850
47	3 Mar 667	110	16 Apr 728	174	20 May 790	237	5 July 851
48	20 Feb 668	111	5 Apr 729	175	10 May 791	238	23 June 852
49	9 Feb 669	112	26 Mar 730	176	28 Apr 792	239	12 June 853
50	29 Jan 670	113	15 Mar 731	177	18 Apr 793	240	2 June 854
51	18 Jan 671	114	3 Mar 732	178	7 Apr 794	241	22 May 855
52	8 Jan 672	115	21 Feb 733	179	27 Mar 795	242	10 May 856
53	27 Dec 672	116	10 Feb 734	180	16 Mar 796	243	30 Apr 857
54	16 Dec 673	117	31 Jan 735	181	5 Mar 797	244	19 Apr 858
55	6 Dec 674	118	20 Jan 736	182	22 Feb 798	245	8 Apr 859
56	25 Nov 675	119	8 Jan 737	183	12 Feb 799	246	28 Mar 860
57	14 Nov 676	120	29 Dec 737			247	17 Mar 861
58	3 Nov 677	121	18 Dec 738	184	1 Feb 800	248	7 Mar 862
59	23 Oct 678	122	7 Dec 739	185	20 Jan 801	249	24 Feb 863
60	13 Oct 679	123	26 Nov 740	186	10 Jan 802	250	13 Feb 864
61	1 Oct 680	124	15 Nov 741	187	30 Dec 802	251	2 Feb 865
62	20 Sept 681	125	4 Nov 742	188	20 Dec 803	252	22 Jan 866
63	10 Sept 682	126	25 Oct 743	189	8 Dec 804	253	11 Jan 867
64	30 Aug 683	127	13 Oct 744	190	27 Nov 805	254	1 Jan 868

Calendar Conversion Table

Hijra Year	Western Date of Muḥarram 1	Hijra Year	Western Date of Muḥarram 1	Hijra Year	Western Date of Muḥarram 1	Hijra Year	Western Date of Muḥarram 1
255	20 Dec 868	318	3 Feb 930	382	9 Mar 992	445	23 Apr 1053
256	9 Dec 869	319	24 Jan 931	383	26 Feb 993	446	12 Apr 1054
257	29 Nov. 870	320	13 Jan 932	384	15 Feb 994	447	2 Apr 1055
258	18 Nov 871	321	1 Jan 933	385	5 Feb 995	448	21 Mar 1056
259	7 Nov 872	322	22 Dec 933	386	25 Jan 996	449	10 Mar 1057
260	27 Oct 873	323	11 Dec 934	387	14 Jan 997	450	28 Feb 1058
261	16 Oct 874	324	30 Nov 935	388	3 Jan 998	451	17 Feb 1059
262	6 Oct 875	325	19 Nov 936	389	23 Dec 998	452	6 Feb 1060
263	24 Sept 876	326	8 Nov 937	390	13 Dec 999	453	26 Jan 1061
264	13 Sept 877	327	29 Oct 938			454	15 Jan 1062
265	3 Sept 878	328	18 Oct 939	391	1 Dec 1000	455	4 Jan 1063
266	23 Aug 879	329	6 Oct 940	392	20 Nov 1001	456	25 Dec 1063
267	12 Aug 880	330	26 Sept 941	393	10 Nov 1002	457	13 Dec 1064
268	1 Aug 881	331	15 Sept 942	394	30 Oct 1003	458	3 Dec 1065
269	21 July 882	332	4 Sept 943	395	18 Oct 1004	459	22 Nov 1066
270	11 July 883	333	24 Aug 944	396	8 Oct 1005	460	11 Nov 1067
271	29 June 884	334	13 Aug 945	397	27 Sept 1006	461	31 Oct 1068
272	18 June 885	335	2 Aug 946	398	17 Sept 1007	462	20 Oct 1069
273	8 June 886	336	23 July 947	399	5 Sept 1008	463	9 Oct 1070
274	28 May 887	337	11 July 948	400	25 Aug 1009	464	29 Sept 1071
275	16 May 888	338	1 July 949	401	15 Aug 1010	465	17 Sept 1072
276	6 May 889	339	20 June 950	402	4 Aug 1011	466	6 Sept 1073
277	25 Apr 890	340	9 June 951	403	23 July 1012	467	27 Aug 1074
278	15 Apr 891	341	29 May 952	404	13 July 1013	468	16 Aug 1075
279	3 Apr 892	342	18 May 953	405	3 July 1014	469	5 Aug 1076
280	23 Mar 893	343	7 May 954	406	21 June 1015	470	25 July 1077
281	13 Mar 094	344	27 Apr 955	407	10 June 1016	471	14 July 1078
282	2 Mar 895	345	15 Apr 956	408	30 May 1017	472	4 July 1079
283	19 Feb 896	346	4 Apr 957	409	20 May 1018	473	22 June 1080
284	8 Feb 897	347	25 Mar 958	410	9 May 1019	474	11 June 1081
285	28 Jan 898	348	14 Mar 959	411	27 Apr 1020	475	1 June 1082
286	17 Jan 899	349	3 Mar 960	412	17 Apr 1021	476	21 May 1083
		350	20 Feb 961	413	6 Apr 1022	477	10 May 1084
287	7 Jan 900	351	9 Feb 962	414	26 Mar 1023	478	29 Apr 1085
288	26 Dec 900	352	30 Jan 963	415	15 Mar 1024	479	18 Apr 1086
289	16 Dec 901	353	19 Jan 964	416	4 Mar 1025	480	8 Apr 1087
290	5 Dec 902	354	7 Jan 965	417	22 Feb 1026	481	27 Mar 1088
291	24 Nov 903	355	28 Dec 965	418	11 Feb 1027	482	16 Mar 1089
292	13 Nov 904	356	17 Dec 966	419	31 Jan 1028	483	6 Mar 1090
293	2 Nov 905	357	7 Dec 967	420	20 Jan 1029	484	23 Feb 1091
294	22 Oct 906	358	25 Nov 968	421	9 Jan 1030	485	12 Feb 1092
295	12 Oct 907	359	14 Nov 969	422	29 Dec 1030	486	1 Feb 1093
296	30 Sept 908	360	4 Nov 970	423	19 Dec 1031	487	21 Jan 1094
297	20 Sept 909	361	24 Oct 971	424	7 Dec 1032	488	11 Jan 1095
298	9 Sept 910	362	12 Oct 972	425	26 Nov 1033	489	31 Dec 1095
299	29 Aug 911	363	2 Oct 973	426	16 Nov 1034	490	19 Dec 1096
300	18 Aug 912	364	21 Sept 974	427	5 Nov 1035	491	9 Dec 1097
301	7 Aug 913	365	10 Sept 975	428	25 Oct 1036	492	28 Nov 1098
302	27 July 914	366	30 Aug 976	429	14 Oct 1037	493	17 Nov 1099
303	17 July 915	367	19 Aug 977	430	3 Oct 1038		
304	5 July 916	368	9 Aug 978	431	23 Sept 1039	494	6 Nov 1100
305	24 June 917	369	29 July 979	432	11 Sept 1040	495	26 Oct 1101
306	14 June 918	370	17 July 980	433	31 Aug 1041	496	15 Oct 1102
307	3 June 919	371	7 July 981	434	21 Aug 1042	497	5 Oct 1103
308	23 May 920	372	26 June 982	435	10 Aug 1043	498	23 Sept 1104
309	12 May 921	373	15 June 983	436	29 July 1044	499	13 Sept 1105
310	1 May 922	374	4 June 984	437	19 July 1045	500	2 Sept 1106
311	21 Apr 923	375	24 May 985	438	8 July 1046	501	22 Aug 1107
312	9 Apr 924	376	13 May 986	439	28 June 1047	502	11 Aug 1108
313	29 Mar 925	377	3 May 987	440	16 June 1048	503	31 July 1109
314	19 Mar 926	378	21 Apr 988	441	5 June 1049	504	20 July 1110
315	8 Mar 927	379	11 Apr 989	442	26 May 1050	505	10 July 1111
316	25 Feb 928	380	31 Mar 990	443	15 May 1051	506	28 June 1112
317	14 Feb 929	381	20 Mar 991	444	3 May 1052	507	18 June 1113

Calendar Conversion Table

Hijra Year	Western Date of Muḥarram 1	Hijra Year	Western Date of Muḥarram 1	Hijra Year	Western Date of Muḥarram 1	Hijra Year	Western Date of Muḥarram 1
508	7 June 1114	572	10 July 1176	635	24 Aug 1237	699	28 Sept 1299
509	27 May 1115	573	30 June 1177	636	14 Aug 1238		
510	16 May 1116	574	19 June 1178	637	3 Aug 1239	700	16 Sept 1300
511	5 May 1117	575	8 June 1179	638	23 July 1240	701	5 Sept 1301
512	24 Apr 1118	576	28 May 1180	639	12 July 1241	702	26 Aug 1302
513	14 Apr 1119	577	17 May 1181	640	1 July 1242	703	15 Aug 1303
514	2 Apr 1120	578	7 May 1182	641	21 June 1243	704	4 Aug 1304
515	22 Mar 1121	579	26 Apr 1183	642	9 June 1244	705	24 July 1305
516	12 Mar 1122	580	14 Apr 1184	643	29 May 1245	706	13 July 1306
517	1 Mar 1123	581	4 Apr 1185	644	19 May 1246	707	3 July 1307
518	19 Feb 1124	582	24 Mar 1186	645	8 May 1247	708	21 June 1308
519	7 Feb 1125	583	13 Mar 1187	646	26 Apr 1248	709	11 June 1309
520	27 Jan 1126	584	2 Mar 1188	647	16 Apr 1249	710	31 May 1310
521	17 Jan 1127	585	19 Feb 1189	648	5 Apr 1250	711	20 May 1311
522	6 Jan 1128	586	8 Feb 1190	649	26 Mar 1251	712	9 May 1312
523	25 Dec 1128	587	29 Jan 1191	650	14 Mar 1252	713	28 Apr 1313
524	15 Dec 1129	588	18 Jan 1192	651	3 Mar 1253	714	17 Apr 1314
525	4 Dec 1130	589	7 Jan 1193	652	21 Feb 1254	715	7 Apr 1315
526	23 Nov 1131	590	27 Dec 1193	653	10 Feb 1255	716	26 Mar 1316
527	12 Nov 1132	591	16 Dec 1194	654	30 Jan 1256	717	16 Mar 1317
528	1 Nov 1133	592	6 Dec 1195	655	19 Jan 1257	718	5 Mar 1318
529	22 Oct 1134	593	24 Nov 1196	656	8 Jan 1258	719	22 Feb 1319
530	11 Oct 1135	594	13 Nov 1197	657	29 Dec 1258	720	12 Feb 1320
531	29 Sept 1136	595	3 Nov 1198	658	18 Dec 1259	721	31 Jan 1321
532	19 Sept 1137	596	23 Oct 1199	659	6 Dec 1260	722	20 Jan 1322
533	8 Sept 1138			660	26 Nov 1261	723	10 Jan 1323
534	28 Aug 1139	597	12 Oct 1200	661	15 Nov 1262	724	30 Dec 1323
535	17 Aug 1140	598	1 Oct 1201	662	4 Nov 1263	725	18 Dec 1324
536	6 Aug 1141	599	20 Sept 1202	663	24 Oct 1264	726	8 Dec 1325
537	27 July 1142	600	10 Sept 1203	664	13 Oct 1265	727	27 Nov 1326
538	16 July 1143	601	29 Aug 1204	665	2 Oct 1266	728	17 Nov 1327
539	4 July 1144	602	18 Aug 1205	666	22 Sept 1267	729	5 Nov 1328
540	24 June 1145	603	8 Aug 1206	667	10 Sept 1268	730	25 Oct 1329
541	13 June 1146	604	28 July 1207	668	31 Aug 1269	731	15 Oct 1330
542	2 June 1147	605	16 July 1208	669	20 Aug 1270	732	4 Oct 1331
543	22 May 1148	606	6 July 1209	670	9 Aug 1271	733	22 Sept 1332
544	11 May 1149	607	25 June 1210	671	29 July 1272	734	12 Sept 1333
545	30 Apr 1150	608	15 June 1211	672	18 July 1273	735	1 Sept 1334
546	20 Apr 1151	609	3 June 1212	673	7 July 1274	736	21 Aug 1335
547	8 Apr 1152	610	23 May 1213	674	27 June 1275	737	10 Aug 1336
548	27 Mar 1153	611	13 May 1214	675	15 June 1276	738	30 July 1337
549	18 Mar 1154	612	2 May 1215	676	4 June 1277	739	20 July 1338
550	7 Mar 1155	613	20 Apr 1216	677	25 May 1278	740	9 July 1339
551	25 Feb 1156	614	10 Apr 1217	678	14 May 1279	741	27 June 1340
552	13 Feb 1157	615	30 Mar 1218	679	3 May 1280	742	17 June 1341
553	2 Feb 1158	616	19 Mar 1219	680	22 Apr 1281	743	6 June 1342
554	23 Jan 1159	617	8 Mar 1220	681	11 Apr 1282	744	26 May 1343
555	12 Jan 1160	618	25 Feb 1221	682	1 Apr 1823	745	15 May 1344
556	31 Dec 1160	619	15 Feb 1222	683	20 Mar 1284	746	4 May 1345
557	21 Dec 1161	620	4 Feb 1223	684	9 Mar 1285	747	24 Apr 1346
558	10 Dec 1162	621	24 Jan 1224	685	27 Feb 1286	748	13 Apr 1347
559	30 Nov 1163	622	13 Jan 1225	686	16 Feb 1287	749	1 Apr 1348
560	18 Nov 1164	623	2 Jan 1226	687	6 Feb 1288	750	22 Mar 1349
561	7 Nov 1165	624	22 Dec 1226	688	25 Jan 1289	751	11 Mar 1350
562	28 Oct 1166	625	12 Dec 1227	689	14 Jan 1290	752	28 Feb 1351
563	17 Oct 1167	626	30 Nov 1228	690	4 Jan 1291	753	18 Feb 1352
564	5 Oct 1168	627	20 Nov 1229	691	24 Dec 1921	754	6 Feb 1353
565	25 Sept 1169	628	9 Nov 1230	692	12 Dec 1292	755	26 Jan 1354
566	14 Sept 1170	629	29 Oct 1231	693	2 Dec 1293	756	16 Jan 1355
567	4 Sept 1171	630	18 Oct 1232	694	21 Nov 1294	757	5 Jan 1356
568	23 Aug 1172	631	7 Oct 1233	695	10 Nov 1295	758	25 Dec 1356
569	12 Aug 1173	632	26 Sept 1234	696	30 Oct 1296	759	15 Dec 1357
570	2 Aug 1174	633	16 Sept 1235	697	19 Oct 1297	760	3 Dec 1358
571	22 July 1175	634	4 Sept 1236	698	9 Oct 1298	761	23 Nov 1359

Calendar Conversion Table

Hijra Year	Western Date of Muḥarram 1	Hijra Year	Western Date of Muḥarram 1	Hijra Year	Western Date of Muḥarram 1	Hijra Year	Western Date of Muḥarram 1
762	11 Nov 1360	825	26 Dec 1421	889	30 Jan 1484	952	15 Mar 1545
763	31 Oct 1361	826	15 Dec 1422	890	18 Jan 1485	953	4 Mar 1546
764	21 Oct 1362	827	5 Dec 1423	891	7 Jan 1486	954	21 Feb 1547
765	10 Oct 1363	828	23 Nov 1424	892	28 Dec 1486	955	11 Feb 1548
766	28 Sept 1364	829	13 Nov 1425	893	17 Dec 1487	956	30 Jan 1549
767	18 Sept 1365	830	2 Nov 1426	894	5 Dec 1488	957	20 Jan 1550
768	7 Sept 1366	831	22 Oct 1427	895	25 Nov 1489	958	9 Jan 1551
769	28 Aug 1367	832	11 Oct 1428	896	14 Nov 1490	959	29 Dec 1551
770	16 Aug 1368	833	30 Sept 1429	897	4 Nov 1491	960	18 Dec 1552
771	5 Aug 1369	834	19 Sept 1430	898	23 Oct 1492	961	7 Dec 1553
772	26 July 1370	835	9 Sept 1431	899	12 Oct 1493	962	26 Nov 1554
773	15 July 1371	836	28 Aug 1432	900	2 Oct 1494	963	16 Nov 1555
774	3 July 1372	837	18 Aug 1433	901	21 Sept 1495	964	4 Nov 1556
775	23 June 1373	838	7 Aug 1434	902	9 Sept 1496	965	24 Oct 1557
776	12 June 1374	839	27 July 1435	903	30 Aug 1497	966	14 Oct 1558
777	2 June 1375	840	16 July 1436	904	19 Aug 1498	967	3 Oct 1559
778	21 May 1376	841	5 July 1437	905	8 Aug 1499	968	22 Sept 1560
779	10 May 1377	842	24 June 1438			969	11 Sept 1561
780	30 Apr 1378	843	14 June 1439	906	28 July 1500	970	31 Aug 1562
781	19 Apr 1379	844	2 June 1440	907	17 July 1501	971	21 Aug 1563
782	7 Apr 1380	845	22 May 1441	908	7 July 1502	972	9 Aug 1564
783	28 Mar 1381	846	12 May 1442	909	26 June 1503	973	29 July 1565
784	17 Mar 1382	847	1 May 1443	910	14 June 1504	974	19 July 1566
785	6 Mar 1383	848	20 Apr 1444	911	4 June 1505	975	8 July 1567
786	24 Feb 1384	849	9 Apr 1445	912	24 May 1506	976	26 June 1568
787	12 Feb 1385	850	29 Mar 1446	913	13 May 1507	977	16 June 1569
788	2 Feb 1386	851	19 Mar 1447	914	2 May 1508	978	5 June 1570
789	22 Jan 1387	852	7 Mar 1448	915	21 Apr 1509	979	26 May 1571
790	11 Jan 1388	853	24 Feb 1449	916	10 Apr 1510	980	14 May 1572
791	31 Dec 1388	854	14 Feb 1450	917	31 Mar 1511	981	3 May 1573
792	20 Dec 1389	855	3 Feb 1451	918	19 Mar 1512	982	23 Apr 1574
793	9 Dec 1390	856	23 Jan 1452	919	9 Mar 1513	983	12 Apr 1575
794	29 Nov 1391	857	12 Jan 1453	920	26 Feb 1514	984	31 Mar 1576
795	17 Nov 1392	858	1 Jan 1454	921	15 Feb 1515	985	21 Mar 1577
796	6 Nov 1393	859	22 Dec 1454	922	5 Feb 1516	986	10 Mar 1578
797	27 Oct 1394	860	11 Dec 1455	923	24 Jan 1517	987	28 Feb 1579
798	16 Oct 1395	861	29 Nov 1456	924	13 Jan 1518	988	17 Feb 1580
799	5 Oct 1396	862	19 Nov 1457	925	3 Jan 1519	989	5 Feb 1581
800	24 Sept 1397	863	8 Nov 1458	926	23 Dec 1519	990	26 Jan 1582
801	13 Sept 1398	864	28 Oct 1459	927	12 Dec 1520	991	25 Jan 1583
802	3 Sept 1399	865	17 Oct 1460	928	1 Dec 1521	992	14 Jan 1584
		866	6 Oct 1461	929	20 Nov 1522	993	3 Jan 1585
803	22 Aug 1400	867	26 Sept 1462	930	10 Nov 1523	994	23 Dec 1585
804	11 Aug 1401	868	15 Sept 1463	931	29 Oct 1524	995	12 Dec 1586
805	1 Aug 1402	869	3 Sept 1464	932	18 Oct 1525	996	2 Dec 1587
806	21 July 1403	870	23 Aug 1465	933	8 Oct 1526	997	20 Nov 1588
807	10 July 1404	871	13 Aug 1466	934	27 Oct 1527	998	10 Nov 1589
808	29 June 1405	872	2 Aug 1467	935	15 Sept 1528	999	30 Oct 1590
809	18 June 1406	873	22 July 1468	936	5 Sept 1529	1000	19 Oct 1591
810	8 June 1407	874	11 July 1469	937	25 Aug 1530		
811	27 May 1408	875	30 June 1470	938	15 Aug 1531	1001	8 Oct 1592
812	16 May 1409	876	20 June 1471	939	3 Aug 1532	1002	27 Sept 1593
813	6 May 1410	877	8 June 1472	940	23 July 1533	1003	16 Sept 1594
814	25 Apr 1411	878	29 May 1473	941	13 July 1534	1004	6 Sept 1595
815	13 Apr 1412	879	18 May 1474	942	2 July 1535	1005	28 Aug 1596
816	3 Apr 1413	880	7 May 1475	943	20 June 1536	1006	14 Aug 1597
817	23 Mar 1414	881	26 Apr 1476	944	10 June 1537	1007	4 Aug 1598
818	13 Mar 1415	882	15 Apr 1477	945	30 May 1538	1008	24 July 1599
819	1 Mar 1416	883	4 Apr 1478	946	19 May 1539		
820	18 Feb 1417	884	25 Mar 1479	947	8 May 1540	1009	13 July 1600
821	8 Feb 1418	885	13 Mar 1480	948	27 Apr 1541	1010	2 July 1601
822	28 Jan 1419	886	2 Mar 1481	949	17 Apr 1542	1011	21 June 1602
823	17 Jan 1420	887	20 Feb 1482	950	6 Apr 1543	1012	11 June 1603
824	6 Jan 1421	888	9 Feb 1483	951	25 Mar 1544	1013	30 May 1604

A MIDDLE EAST STUDIES HANDBOOK

Calendar Conversion Table

Hijra Year	Western Date of Muḥarram 1	Hijra Year	Western Date of Muḥarram 1	Hijra Year	Western Date od Muḥarram 1	Hijra Year	Western Date of Muḥarram 1
1014	19 May 1605	1078	23 June 1667	1141	7 Aug 1728	1205	10 Sept 1790
1015	9 May 1606	1079	11 June 1668	1142	27 July 1729	1206	31 Aug 1791
1016	28 Apr 1607	1080	1 June 1669	1143	17 July 1730	1207	19 Aug 1792
1017	17 Apr 1608	1081	21 May 1670	1144	6 July 1731	1208	9 Aug 1793
1018	6 Apr 1609	1082	10 May 1671	1145	24 June 1732	1209	29 July 1794
1019	26 Mar 1610	1083	29 Apr 1672	1146	14 June 1733	1210	18 July 1795
1020	16 Mar 1611	1084	18 Apr 1673	1147	3 June 1734	1211	7 July 1796
1021	4 Mar 1612	1085	7 Apr 1674	1148	24 May 1735	1212	26 June 1797
1022	21 Feb 1613	1086	28 Mar 1675	1149	12 May 1736	1213	15 June 1798
1023	11 Feb 1614	1087	16 Mar 1676	1150	1 May 1737	1214	5 June 1799
1024	31 Jan 1615	1088	6 Mar 1677	1151	21 Apr 1738		
1025	20 Jan 1616	1089	23 Feb 1678	1152	10 Apr 1739	1215	25 May 1800
1026	9 Jan 1617	1090	12 Feb 1679	1153	29 Mar 1740	1216	14 May 1801
1027	29 Dec 1617	1091	2 Feb 1680	1154	19 Mar 1741	1217	4 May 1802
1028	19 Dec 1618	1092	21 Jan 1681	1155	8 Mar 1742	1218	23 Apr 1803
1029	8 Dec 1619	1093	10 Jan 1682	1156	25 Feb 1743	1219	12 Apr 1804
1030	26 Nov 1620	1094	31 Dec 1682	1157	15 Feb 1744	1220	1 Apr 1805
1031	16 Nov 1621	1095	20 Dec 1683	1158	3 Feb 1745	1221	21 Mar 1806
1032	5 Nov 1622	1096	8 Dec 1684	1159	24 Jan 1746	1222	11 Mar 1807
1033	25 Oct 1623	1097	28 Nov 1685	1160	13 Jan 1747	1223	28 Feb 1808
1034	14 Oct 1624	1098	17 Nov 1686	1161	2 Jan 1748	1224	16 Feb 1809
1035	3 Oct 1625	1099	7 Nov 1687	1162	22 Dec 1748	1225	6 Feb 1810
1036	22 Sept 1626	1100	26 Oct 1688	1163	11 Dec 1749	1226	26 Jan 1811
1037	12 Sept 1627	1101	15 Oct 1689	1164	30 Nov 1750	1227	16 Jan 1812
1038	31 Aug 1638	1102	5 Oct 1690	1165	20 Nov 1751	1228	4 Jan 1813
1039	21 Aug 1629	1103	24 Sept 1691	1166	8 Nov 1752	1229	24 Dec 1813
1040	10 Aug 1630	1104	12 Sept 1692	1167	29 Oct 1753	1230	14 Dec 1814
1041	30 July 1631	1105	2 Sept 1693	1168	18 Oct 1754	1231	3 Dec 1815
1042	19 July 1632	1106	22 Aug 1694	1169	7 Oct 1755	1232	21 Nov 1816
1043	8 July 1633	1107	12 Aug 1695	1170	26 Sept 1756	1233	11 Nov 1817
1044	27 June 1634	1108	31 July 1696	1171	15 Sept 1757	1234	31 Oct 1818
1045	17 June 1635	1109	20 July 1697	1172	4 Sept 1758	1235	20 Oct 1819
1046	5 June 1636	1110	10 July 1698	1173	25 Aug 1759	1236	9 Oct 1820
1047	26 May 1637	1111	29 June 1699	1174	13 Aug 1760	1237	28 Sept 1821
1048	15 May 1638			1175	2 Aug 1761	1238	18 Sept 1822
1049	4 May 1639	1112	18 June 1700	1176	23 July 1762	1239	7 Sept 1823
1050	23 Apr 1640	1113	8 June 1701	1177	12 July 1763	1240	26 Aug 1824
1051	12 Apr 1641	1114	28 May 1702	1178	1 July 1764	1241	16 Aug 1825
1052	1 Apr 1642	1115	17 May 1703	1179	20 June 1765	1242	5 Aug 1826
1053	22 Mar 1643	1116	6 May 1704	1180	9 June 1766	1243	25 July 1827
1054	10 Mar 1644	1117	25 Apr 1705	1181	30 May 1767	1244	14 July 1828
1055	27 Feb 1645	1118	15 Apr 1706	1182	18 May 1768	1245	3 July 1829
1056	17 Feb 1646	1119	4 Apr 1707	1183	7 May 1769	1246	22 June 1830
1057	6 Feb 1647	1120	23 Mar 1708	1184	27 Apr 1770	1247	12 June 1831
1058	27 Jan 1648	1121	13 Mar 1709	1185	16 Apr 1771	1248	31 May 1832
1059	15 Jan 1649	1122	2 Mar 1710	1186	4 Apr 1772	1249	21 May 1833
1060	4 Jan 1650	1123	19 Feb 1711	1187	25 Mar 1773	1250	10 May 1834
1061	25 Dec 1650	1124	9 Feb 1712	1188	14 Mar 1774	1251	29 Apr 1835
1062	14 Dec 1651	1125	28 Jan 1713	1189	4 Mar 1775	1252	18 Apr 1836
1063	2 Dec 1652	1126	17 Jan 1714	1190	21 Feb 1776	1253	7 Apr 1837
1064	22 Nov 1653	1127	7 Jan 1715	1191	19 Feb 1777	1254	27 Mar 1838
1065	11 Nov 1654	1128	27 Dec 1715	1192	30 Jan 1778	1255	17 Mar 1839
1066	31 Oct 1655	1129	16 Dec 1716	1193	19 Jan 1779	1256	5 Mar 1840
1067	20 Oct 1656	1130	5 Dec 1717	1194	8 Jan 1780	1257	23 Feb 1841
1068	9 Oct 1657	1131	24 Nov 1718	1195	28 Dec 1780	1258	12 Feb 1842
1069	29 Sept 1658	1132	14 Nov 1719	1196	17 Dec 1781	1259	1 Feb 1843
1070	18 Sept 1659	1133	2 Nov 1720	1197	7 Dec 1782	1260	22 Jan 1844
1071	6 Sept 1660	1134	22 Oct 1721	1198	26 Nov 1783	1261	10 Jan 1845
1072	27 Aug 1661	1135	12 Oct 1722	1199	14 Nov 1784	1262	30 Dec 1845
1073	16 Aug 1662	1136	1 Oct 1723	1200	4 Nov 1785	1263	20 Dec 1846
1074	5 Aug 1663	1137	20 Sept 1724	1201	24 Oct 1786	1264	9 Dec 1847
1075	25 July 1664	1138	9 Sept 1725	1202	13 Oct 1787	1265	27 Nov 1848
1076	14 July 1665	1139	29 Aug 1726	1203	2 Oct 1788	1266	17 Nov 1849
1077	4 July 1666	1140	19 Aug 1727	1204	21 Sept 1789	1267	6 Nov 1850

Calendar Conversion Table

Hijra Year	Western Date of Muḥarram 1	Hijra Year	Western Date of Muḥarram 1	Hijra Year	Western Date of Muḥarram 1	Hijra Year	Western Date of Muḥarram 1
1268	27 Oct 1851	1331	11 Dec 1912	1395	14 Jan 1975		
1269	15 Oct 1852	1332	30 Nov 1913	1396	3 Jan 1976		
1270	4 Oct 1853	1333	19 Nov 1914	1397	23 Dec 1976		
1271	24 Sept 1854	1334	9 Nov 1915	1398	12 Dec 1977		
1272	13 Sept 1855	1335	28 Oct 1916	1399	2 Dec 1978		
1273	1 Sept 1856	1336	17 Oct 1917	1400	21 Nov 1979		
1274	22 Aug 1857	1337	7 Oct 1918	1401	9 Nov 1980		
1275	11 Aug 1858	1338	26 Sept 1919	1402	30 Oct 1981		
1276	31 July 1859	1339	15 Sept 1920	1403	19 Oct 1982		
1277	20 July 1860	1340	4 Sept 1921	1404	8 Oct 1983		
1278	9 July 1861	1341	24 Aug 1922	1405	27 Sept 1984		
1279	29 June 1862	1342	14 Aug 1923	1406	16 Sept 1985		
1280	18 June 1863	1343	2 Aug 1924	1407	6 Sept 1986		
1281	6 June 1864	1344	22 July 1925	1408	26 Aug 1987		
1282	27 May 1865	1345	12 July 1926	1409	14 Aug 1988		
1283	16 May 1866	1346	1 July 1927	1410	4 Aug 1989		
1284	5 May 1867	1347	20 June 1928	1411	24 July 1990		
1285	24 Apr 1868	1348	9 June 1929	1412	13 July 1991		
1286	13 Apr 1869	1349	29 May 1930	1413	2 July 1992		
1287	3 Apr 1870	1350	19 May 1931	1414	21 June 1993		
1288	23 Mar 1871	1351	7 May 1932	1415	10 June 1994		
1289	11 Mar 1872	1352	26 Apr 1933	1416	31 May 1995		
1290	1 Mar 1873	1353	16 Apr 1934	1417	19 May 1996		
1291	18 Feb 1874	1354	5 Apr 1935	1418	9 May 1997		
1292	7 Feb 1875	1355	24 Mar 1936	1419	28 Apr 1998		
1293	28 Jan 1876	1356	14 Mar 1937	1420	17 Apr 1999		
1294	16 Jan 1877	1357	3 Mar 1938				
1295	5 Jan 1878	1358	21 Feb 1939	1421	6 Apr 2000		
1296	26 Dec 1878	1359	10 Feb 1940				
1297	15 Dec 1879	1360	29 Jan 1941				
1298	4 Dec 1880	1361	19 Jan 1942				
1299	23 Nov 1881	1362	8 Jan 1943				
1300	12 Nov 1882	1363	28 Dec 1943				
1301	2 Nov 1882	1364	17 Dec 1944				
1302	21 Oct 1884	1365	6 Dec 1945				
1303	10 Oct 1885	1366	25 Nov 1946				
1304	30 Sept 1886	1367	15 Nov 1947				
1305	19 Sept 1887	1368	3 Nov 1948				
1306	7 Sept 1888	1369	24 Oct 1949				
1307	28 Aug 1889	1370	13 Oct 1950				
1308	17 Aug 1890	1371	2 Oct 1951				
1309	7 Aug 1891	1372	21 Sept 1952				
1310	26 July 1892	1373	10 Sept 1953				
1311	15 July 1893	1374	30 Aug 1954				
1312	5 July 1894	1375	20 Aug 1955				
1313	24 June 1895	1376	8 Aug 1956				
1314	12 June 1896	1377	29 July 1957				
1315	2 June 1897	1378	18 July 1958				
1316	22 May 1898	1379	7 July 1959				
1317	12 May 1899	1380	25 June 1960				
		1381	14 June 1961				
1318	1 May 1900	1382	4 June 1962				
1319	20 May 1901	1383	25 May 1963				
1320	10 Apr 1902	1384	13 May 1964				
1321	30 Mar 1903	1385	2 May 1965				
1322	18 Mar 1904	1386	22 Apr 1966				
1323	8 Mar 1905	1387	11 Apr 1967				
1324	25 Feb 1906	1388	31 May 1968				
1325	14 Feb 1907	1389	20 Mar 1969				
1326	4 Feb 1908	1390	9 Mar 1970				
1327	23 Jan 1909	1391	27 Feb 1971				
1328	13 Jan 1910	1392	16 Feb 1972				
1329	2 Jan 1911	1393	4 Feb 1973				
1330	22 Dec 1911	1394	25 Jan 1974				

IV. Dynasties, Rulers, Administrators

A critical tool for any analysis of political developments is the list of caliphs, sultans, governors, presidents, prime ministers, etc. who ruled over Southwest Asia and Egypt. Students of pre-20th-century Islamic history are very fortunate to have the excellent work by C.E. Bosworth, *The Islamic Dynasties* (Edinburgh: Edinburgh University Press, 1967; 2nd ed., 1980), University of Edinburgh Islamic Surveys, No. 5. In 82 tables, Professor Bosworth lists every major and many minor dynasties from Spain through India. Each section lists the rulers, their regnal dates (in Muslim and Western years), and then presents a brief historical sketch, followed by a few pertinent references. The only weakness of this well-written and fully indexed work is its lack of any genealogical tables.

If one wishes more extensive tables of rulers and genealogical tables for medieval Islamic history — including numerous lists of *wazīr*s and governors, full Muslim dates for the beginning of a rule and, when possible, Muslim dates of death — the best source is Edward von Zambaur, *Manuel de Généalogie et de Chronologie pour l'Histoire de l'Islam* (Hanover, 1927 [reprinted in Berlin, 1955]. There is also an Arabic translation of Zambaur by Zaki M. Ḥasan Bey, Ḥasan Aḥmad Maḥmūd and others, *Muᶜjam al-Ansāb wa'l-Usarāt al-Hakīma fī'l-Ta'rīkh al-Islāmī* (Cairo: Arab League, 1370/1951). However, unlike Bosworth, neither Zambaur nor the translation of his work includes Western dates, historical summaries or a bibliography.

One other important source of information on medieval dynasties, *wazīr*s, etc. is *EI*[1] and *EI*[2]. Stanley Lane-Poole's pioneer work, *The Mohammaden Dynasties* (London, 1893 [reprinted New York: Frederick Ungar Publishing Co., 1965]), includes dynasties not in Bosworth and genealogical tables. A.D. Alderson, *The Structure of the Ottoman Dynasty* (Oxford: Clarendon Press, 1956), is the best Western source for data related to the Ottoman family.

A recent reference work in Arabic is by Dr. Aḥmad al-Saᶜīd Sulaymān, entitled *Ta'rīkh al-Duwal al-Islāmiyya wa Muᶜjam al-Usar al-Hakīma* (Cairo: Dār al-Maᶜārif [n.d.]). His book includes 115 dynasties with a brief historical introduction, the names and dates of the rulers and, whenever possible, a genealogy table. His dates for Iranian dynasties often differ from those found in Western sources.

The material which follows has been arranged in the following manner: general divisions with a list of the dates of the dynasties (and a few other groups) which ruled in that area for the period covered. Those dynasties, ministers, officials marked by "*" are broken down into a list of the individuals with the dates they were in power, and those categories marked with a "+" are presented in the form of a genealogical table. The choice of those groups given in greater detail or in a genealogical table reflect my teaching experience and are not meant to be comprehensive.

CALIPHS AND WAZĪRS

			Muslim Dates	Christian Dates
*+	A.	Rāshidūn	11 - 40 A.H.	632 - 661 A.D.
*+	B.	Umayyads	41 - 132	661 - 750
*+	C.1.	^CAbbāsids in Iraq	132 - 656	750 - 1258
*+	2.	Barmakids	ca. 165 - 221	ca. 781 - 835
*	3.	^CAbbāsids in Egypt	659 - 923	1261 - 1517
*+	D.	Selected Early Shī^Cites	35 - c.264	656 - ca. 878

A. Rāshidūn

11/632	Abū Bakr	23/644	^CUthmān b. ^CAffān
13/634	^CUmar b. al-Khaṭṭāb	35-40/656-661	^CAlī b. Abī-Ṭālib

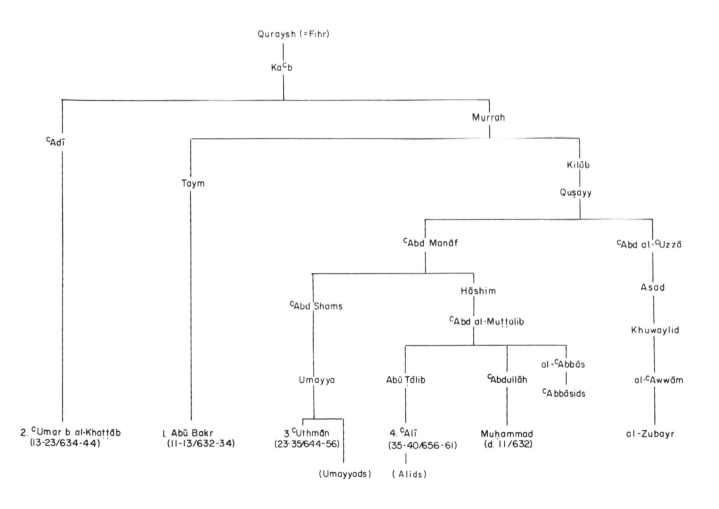

B. Umayyad Caliphs

41/661	Mu^cāwiya I	86/705	al-Walīd I	125/743	al-Walīd II
60/680	Yazīd I	96/715	Sulaymān	126/744	Yazīd III
64/683	Mu^cāwiya II	99/717	^cUmar II	126/744	Ibrāhīm
64/684	Marwān I	101/720	Yazīd II		
65/685	^cAbd al-Malik	105/724	Hishām	127-132/744-750	Marwān II

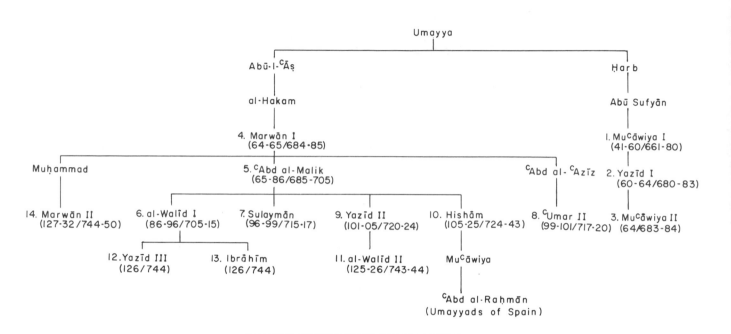

C.1. ^cAbbāsids in Iraq

132/749	al-Saffāḥ	255/869	al-Muhtadī	422/1031	al-Qā'im
136/754	al-Manṣūr	256/870	al-Mu^ctamid	467/1075	al-Muqtadī
158/775	al-Mahdī	279/892	al-Mu^ctaḍid	487/1094	al-Mustaẓhir
169/785	al-Hādī	289/902	al-Muktafī	512/1118	al-Mustarshid
170/786	Hārūn al-Rashīd	295/908	al-Muqtadir	529/1135	al-Rāshid
193/809	al-Amīn	320/932	al-Qāhir	530/1136	al-Muqtafī
198/813	al-Ma'mūn	322/934	al-Rāḍī	555/1160	al-Mustanjid
218/833	al-Mu^ctaṣim	329/940	al-Muttaqī	566/1170	al-Mustaḍī'
227/842	al-Wāthiq	333/944	al-Mustakfī	575/1180	al-Nāṣir
232/847	al-Mutawakkil	334/946	al-Muṭī^c	622/1225	al-Ẓāhir
247/861	al-Muntaṣir	363/974	al-Ṭā'i^c	623/1226	al-Mustanṣir
248/862	al-Musta^cīn	381/991	al-Qādir	640-656/1242-1258	al-Musta^cṣim
252/866	al-Mu^ctazz				

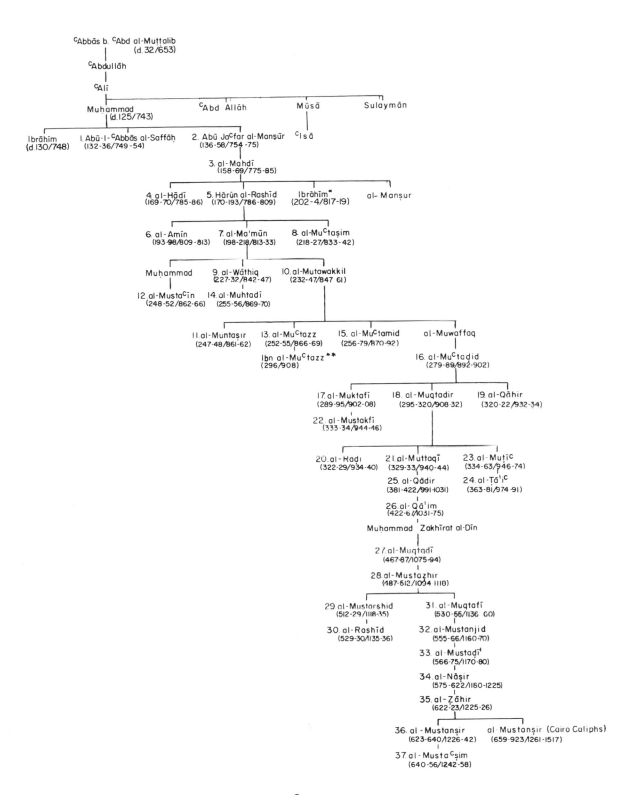

ᶜAbbās b. ᶜAbd al-Muṭṭalib
(d. 32/653)

ᶜAbdullāh

ᶜAlī

Muhammad   ᶜAbd Allāh   Mūsā   Sulaymān
(d.125/743)

Ibrāhīm   I. Abū-l-ᶜAbbās al-Saffāḥ   2. Abū Jaᶜfar al-Manṣūr   ᶜĪsā
(d.130/748)   (132-36/749-54)   (136-58/754-75)

3. al-Mahdī
(158-69/775-85)

4. al-Hādī   5. Hārūn al-Rashīd   Ibrāhīm*   al-Mansūr
(169-70/785-86)   (170-193/786-809)   (202-4/817-19)

6. al-Amīn   7. al-Ma'mūn   8. al-Muᶜtaṣim
(193-98/809-813)   (198-218/813-33)   (218-27/833-42)

Muhammad   9. al-Wāthiq   10. al-Mutawakkil
(227-32/842-47)   (232-47/847 61)

12. al-Mustaᶜīn   14. al-Muhtadī
(248-52/862-66)   (255-56/869-70)

11. al-Muntaṣir   13. al-Muᶜtazz   15. al-Muᶜtamid   al-Muwaffaq
(247-48/861-62)   (252-55/866-69)   (256-79/870-92)

Ibn al-Muᶜtazz**   16. al-Muᶜtadid
(296/908)   (279-89/892-902)

17. al-Muktafī   18. al-Muqtadir   19. al-Qāhir
(289-95/902-08)   (295-320/908-32)   (320-22/932-34)

22. al-Mustakfī
(333-34/944-46)

20. al-Rāḍī   21. al-Muttaqī   23. al-Muṭīᶜ
(322-29/934-40)   (329-33/940-44)   (334-63/946-74)

25. al-Qādir   24. al-Tā'iᶜ
(381-422/991-1031)   (363-81/974-91)

26. al-Qā'im
(422-6/1031-75)

Muhammad Zakhīrat al-Dīn

27. al-Muqtadī
(467-87/1075-94)

28. al-Mustaẓhir
(487-512/1094 1118)

29. al-Mustarshid   31. al-Muqtafī
(512-29/1118-35)   (530-55/1136 60)

30. al-Rashīd   32. al-Mustanjid
(529-30/1135-36)   (555-66/1160-70)

33. al-Mustaḍī'
(566-75/1170-80)

34. al-Nāṣir
(575-622/1180-1225)

35. al-Ẓāhir
(622-23/1225-26)

36. al-Mustanṣir   al-Mustanṣir (Cairo Caliphs)
(623-640/1226-42)   (659-923/1261-1517)

37. al-Mustaᶜṣim
(640-56/1242-58)

IV ᶜABBĀSIDS
(132-650/749-1258)

* In Baghdad

** Caliph for part of a day

C.2. Barmakids

	Barmak		
d. 165/781	Khālid	d. 187/803	Ja^cfar
d. 190/805	Yahyā	d. 193/808	al-Fadl
		d. 221/835	Mūsā

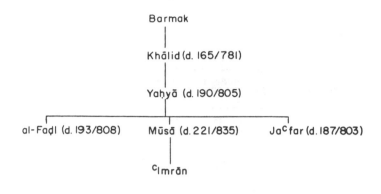

```
                        Barmak
                          |
                   Khālid (d. 165/781)
                          |
                   Yahyā (d. 190/805)
        ┌─────────────────┼─────────────────┐
 al-Fadl (d. 193/808)  Mūsā (d. 221/835)  Ja cfar (d. 187/803)
                          |
                      cImrān
```

C.3. ^CAbbāsids in Egypt

659/1261	al-Mustansir	791/1389	al-Mutawakkil I [3rd reign]
660/1261	al-Hākim I	808/1406	al-Musta^cīn
701/1302	al-Mustakfī I	816/1414	al-Mu^ctadid II
740/1340	al-Wāthiq I	845/1441	al-Mustakfī II
741/1341	al-Hākim II	855/1451	al-Qā'im
753/1352	al-Mu^ctadid I	859/1455	al-Mustanjid
763/1362	al-Mutawakkil I [1st reign]	884/1479	al-Mutawakkil II
779/1377	al-Mu^ctasim [1st reign]	903/1497	al-Mustamsik [1st reign]
779/1377	al-Mutawakkil I [2nd reign]	914/1508	al-Mutawakkil III [1st reign]
785/1383	al-Wāthiq II	922/1516	al-Mustamsik [2nd reign]
788/1385	al-Mu^ctasim [2nd reign]	923/1517	al-Mutawakkil III [2nd reign]

D. Selected Early Shī^cites

d. 40/661	^CAlī	d. 183/799	Mūsā al-Kāzim
d.c. 49/669	Hasan	d. 203/818	^CAlī al-Ridā
d. 61/680	Husayn	d. 220/835	Muhammad al-Jawād
d. 94/712	^CAlī Zayn al-^CĀbidīn	d. 254/868	^CAlī al-Hādī
d. 113/731	Muhammad al-Bāqir	d. 260/874	Hasan al-^CAskarī
d. 148/765	Ja^cfar al-Sādiq	d.c. 264/878	Muhammad al-Mantazar [al-Mahdī]

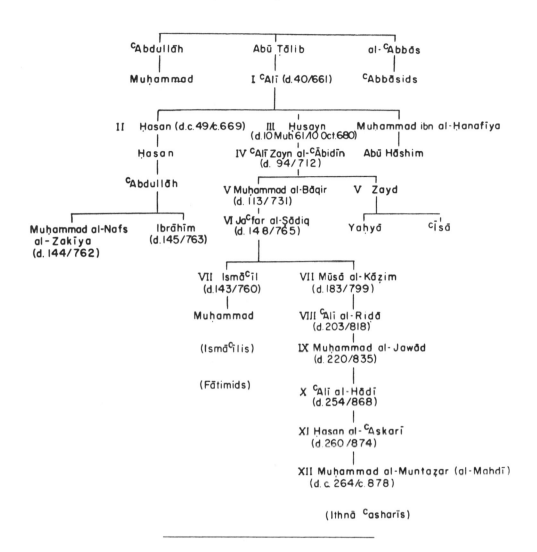

(Ithnā ^casharīs)

E G Y P T

		Muslim Dates	Christian Dates
*+	A. Ṭūlūnids	254 - 292 A.H.	868 - 905 A.D.
*+	B. Ikhshīdids	323 - 358	935 - 969
*+	C. Fāṭimids	297 - 567	909 - 1171
	D. Ayyūbids, including Syria, Iraq and Yemen:	564 - 9th C.	1169 - 15th C.
*+	1. Egypt	564 - 650	1169 - 1252
*	2. Damascus	582 - 658	1186 - 1260
*	3. Aleppo	579 - 658	1183 - 1260
	4. Mayyāfāriqīn, Sinjār	581 - 658	1185 - 1260
	5. Ba^clbakk	568 - 658	1172 - 1260
	6. Hama	574 - 732	1178 - 1332
	7. Ḥimṣ	574 - 661	1178 - 1262
*	8. Yemen	569 - 626	1174 - 1229
	9. Ḥisn Kayfā and Āmid	629 - 9th C.	1232 - 15th C.

[continued]

	Muslim Dates	Christian Dates
E. Mamlūks:	648 - 922 A.H.	1250 - 1517 A.D.
* 1. Baḥrī	648 - 792	1250 - 1390
* 2. Circassian (Burji)	784 - 922	1382 - 1517
*+ F. Muḥammad ^CAlī's Family	1220 - 1372	1805 - 1953
* G. British Consul Generals, High Commissioners	-- --	1879 - 1936
* H. Presidents of Egypt	-- --	1953 -

A. Ṭūlūnids

254/868	Aḥmad b. Ṭūlūn	283/896	Hārūn
270/884	Khumārawayh	292/905	Shaybān
282/896	Jaysh		

B. Ikhshīdids

323/935	Muḥammad b. Ṭughj al-Ikhshīd	355/966	Kāfūr
334/946	Ūnūjūr	357-358/968-969	Aḥmad
349/960	^CAlī		

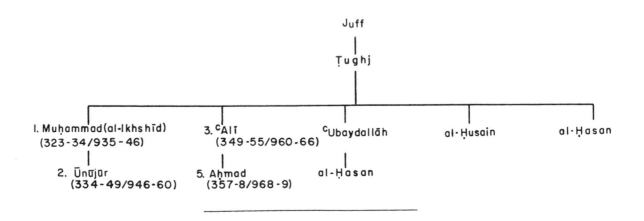

C. Fātimids

297/909	^CUbaydullāh al-Mahdī	386/996	al-Ḥakim	524/1130	Interregnum
322/934	al-Qā'im	411/1021	al-Ẓāhir	525/1131	al-Ḥāfiẓ
334/946	al-Manṣūr	427/1036	al-Mustanṣir	544/1149	al-Ẓāfir
341/953	al-Mu^cizz	487/1094	al-Musta^clī	549/1154	al-Fā'iz
365/975	al-^CAzīz	495/1101	al-Āmir	555-567/1160-1171	al-^CĀḍid

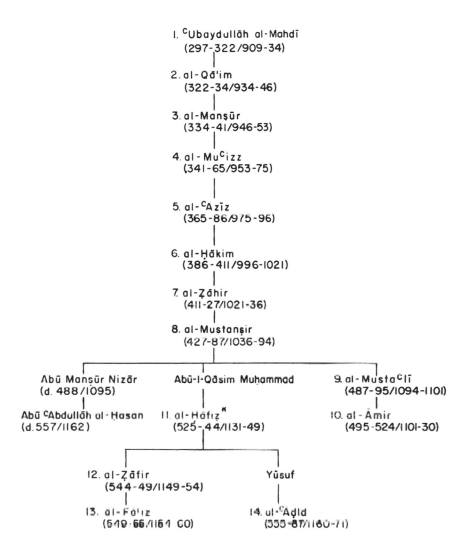

I. ^CUbaydullāh al-Mahdī
(297-322/909-34)

2. al-Qā'im
(322-34/934-46)

3. al-Manṣūr
(334-41/946-53)

4. al-Mu^cizz
(341-65/953-75)

5. al-^CAzīz
(365-86/975-96)

6. al-Ḥākim
(386-411/996-1021)

7. al-Ẓāhir
(411-27/1021-36)

8. al-Mustanṣir
(427-87/1036-94)

Abū Manṣūr Nizār   Abū-l-Qāsim Muḥammad   9. al-Musta^clī
(d. 488/1095)   (487-95/1094-1101)

Abū ^cAbdullāh al-Ḥasan   II. al-Ḥāfiẓ*   10. al-Āmir
(d.557/1162)   (525-44/1131-49)   (495-524/1101-30)

12. al-Ẓāfir   Yūsuf
(544-49/1149-54)

13. al-Fā'iz   14. al-^CĀḍid
(549-55/1154-60)   (555-67/1160-71)

* Interregnum (524-25/1130-31)

D.1 Ayyūbids in Egypt

564/1169	al-Malik al-Nāṣir Ṣalāḥ al-Dīn [Saladin]	635/1238	al-Malik al-^CĀdil II
589/1193	al-Malik al-^CAzīz	637/1240	al-Malik al-Ṣāliḥ Najm al-Dīn Ayyūb
595/1198	al-Malik al-Manṣūr		
596/1200	al-Malik al-^CĀdil I	647/1249	al-Malik al-Mu^caẓẓam Tūrān Shāh
615/1218	al-Malik al-Kāmil	648-50/1250-52	al-Malik al-Ashraf II

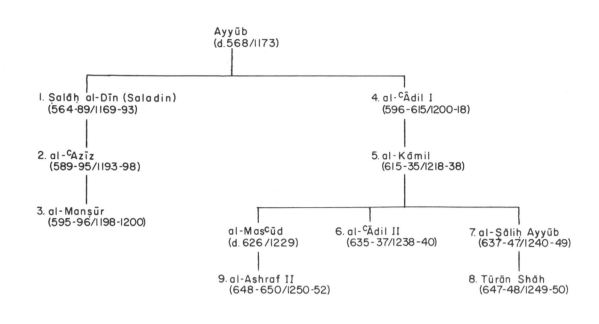

D.2. Ayyūbids in Damascus

582/1186	al-Malik al-Afḍal	635/1238	al-Malik al-ᶜĀdil II
592/1196	al-Malik al-ᶜĀdil I	636/1239	al-Malik al-Ṣāliḥ Najm al-Dīn Ayyūb [1st reign]
615/1218	al-Malik al-Muᶜaẓẓam		
624/1227	al-Malik al-Nāṣir Ṣalāḥ al-Dīn Dā'ūd	637/1239	al-Malik al-Ṣāliḥ Ismāᶜīl [2nd reign]
626/1229	al-Malik al-Ashraf	643/1245	al-Malik al-Ṣāliḥ Najm al-Dīn Ayyūb [2nd reign]
634/1237	al-Malik al-Ṣāliḥ Ismāᶜīl [1st reign]		
		647/1249	al-Malik al-Muᶜaẓẓam Tūrān Shāh
635/1238	al-Malik al-Kāmil	648-58/1250-60	al-Malik al-Nāṣir Ṣalāḥ al-Dīn II

D.3. Ayyūbids in Aleppo

579/1183	al-Malik al-ᶜĀdil I	613/1216	al-Malik al-ᶜAzīz Ghiyāth al-Dīn
582/1186	al-Malik al-Ẓāhir Ghiyāth al-Dīn	634-58/1237-60	al-Malik al-Nāṣir Ṣalāḥ al-Dīn II

D.8. Ayyūbids in Yemen

569/1174	al-Malik al-Muᶜaẓẓam Shams al-Dīn Tūrān Shāh	598/1202	al-Malik al-Nāṣir Ayyūb
		611/1214	al-Malik al-Muẓaffar Sulaymān
577/1181	al-Malik al-ᶜAzīz Ẓāhir al-Dīn Tughtigīn	612-26/1215-29	al-Malik al-Masᶜūd Ṣalāḥ al-Dīn
593/1197	Muᶜizz al-Dīn Ismāᶜīl		

Note: On other branches, see Bosworth and Zambaur.

E.1. Mamlūks - Baḥrī

648/1250	Shajar al-Durr	694/1295	Kitbughā	747/1346	Ḥājjī I
648/1250	Aybak	696/1297	Lājīn	748/1347	al-Nāṣir al-Ḥasan [1st reign]
655/1257	ᶜAlī	698/1299	al-Nāṣir Muḥammad [2nd reign]	752/1351	Ṣāliḥ
657/1259	Quṭuz	708/1309	Baybars II	755/1354	al-Nāṣir al-Ḥasan [2nd reign]
658/1260	Baybars I	709/1309	al-Nāṣir Muḥammad [3rd reign]	762/1361	al-Manṣūr Muḥammad
676/1277	Baraka Khān	741/1340	Abū Bakr	764/1363	Shaᶜbān II
678/1280	Salāmish	742/1341	Kūjūk	778/1376	al-Manṣūr ᶜAlī
678/1280	Qalā'ūn	743/1342	Aḥmad	783/1382	al-Ṣāliḥ Ḥājjī II
689/1290	Khalīl	743/1342	Ismāᶜīl	[784/1382	Barqūq]
693/1294	al-Nāṣir Muḥammad [1st reign]	746/1345	Shaᶜbān I	791/1389	Ḥājjī II [2nd reign]

E.2. Mamlūks - Circassian (Burji)

784/1382	Barqūq [1st reign]	824/1421	Ṭaṭar	872/1467	Bilbay
[791/1389	Ḥājjī II]	824/1421	al-Ṣāliḥ Muḥammad	872/1468	Timurbughā
792/1390	Barqūq [2nd reign]	825/1422	Barsbay	872/1468	al-Ashraf Qāyitbāy
801/1399	Faraj [1st reign]	841/1437	Yūsuf	901/1496	al-Nāṣir Muḥammad
808/1405	al-Manṣūr ᶜAbd al-ᶜAzīz	842/1438	al-Ẓāhir Jaqmaq	903/1498	Qānṣūh
		857/1453	ᶜUthmān	905/1500	Jānbalāt
808/1405	Faraj [2nd reign]	857/1453	Ināl	906/1501	al-ᶜĀdil Tūmān Bay
815/1412	al-ᶜĀdil al-Mustaᶜīn	865/1461	al-Mu'ayyad Aḥmad	906/1501	Qānṣūh al-Ghawrī
815/1412	al-Mu'ayyad Shaykh	865/1461	Khūshqadam	922/1517	al-Ashraf Tūmān Bay
824/1421	al-Muẓaffar Aḥmad				

F. Muhammad ᶜAlī's Family

1220/1805	Muḥammad ᶜAlī Pāshā	1309/1892	ᶜAbbās II Hilmī
1264/1848	Ibrāhīm Pāshā	1333/1914	Ḥusayn Kāmil [Sulṭān]
1264/1848	ᶜAbbās Pāshā	1335/1917	Aḥmad Fu'ād I [King from 1340/1922]
1270/1854	Saᶜīd Pāshā		
1280/1863	Ismāᶜīl [Khedive from 1284/1867]	1355/1936	Fārūq
		1371-72/1952-53	Fu'ād II
1296/1879	Tawfīq		

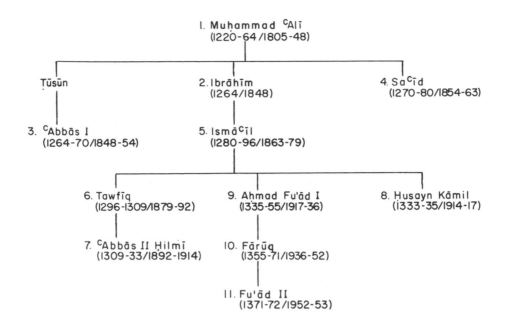

G. <u>British Consul Generals, High Commissioners</u>
   <u>for Egypt, 1879-1936</u>

   1. <u>Consul Generals</u>

1879	Sir Edward Malet	1907	Sir Eldon Gorst
1883	Evelyn Baring [Lord Cromer]	1911	**Lord Herbert Kitchener**

   2. <u>High Commissioners</u>

1914	Sir Henry MacMahon	1925	Lord George Lloyd
1916	Sir Reginald Wingate	1929	Sir Percy Loraine
1919	Sir Edmund Allenby	1933-36	Sir Miles Lampson [Lord Killearn]

H. <u>Presidents of Egypt, 1953-</u>

1953	Muḥammad Nagīb
1954	Gamal ᶜAbd al-Nāṣir
1971	Anwar al-Sādāt
1981	Ḥusnī Mubārak

III. ARABIAN PENINSULA

		Muslim Dates	Christian Dates
	A. Ziyādids	204 - 409 A.H.	819 - 1018 A.D.
	B. Ya^{C}furids	247 - 387	861 - 997
	C. Qarāmiṭa	281 - 5th C.	894 - 11th C.
	D. Zuray'ids	476 - 569	1083 - 1173
	E. Najāḥids	412 - 551	1021 - 1156
	F. Mahdids	554 - 569	1159 - 1173
*	G. Ṣulayḥids [Yemen]	439 - 532	1047 - 1138
	H. Hamdānids of Ṣan^{C}ā'	492 - 569	1098 - 1173
	I. Ayyūbids	[See II, Egypt]	-- --
*	J. Rasūlids [Yemen]	626 - 858	1229 - 1454
	K. Ṭāhirids [Yemen]	850 - 923	1446 - 1517
	L. Rassid Zaydī Imāms	246 - 680	860 - 1281
*	M. Qāsimid Zaydī Imāms [Modern Period]	1000 - 1382	1592 - 1962
	N. Āl Bū Sa^{C}īd	1154 -	1741 -
	O. Rashīdids	1248 - 1342	1832 - 1923
*+	P. Sa^{C}ūdī Family	1159 -	1746 -

G. Ṣulayḥids [Yemen]

439/1047	^{C}Alī b. Muḥammad	484/1091	al-Manṣūr Sabā'
459/1067	al-Mukarram Aḥmad	492-532/1099-1138	al-Sayyida Arwā
477/1084	al-Mukarram ^{C}Alī		

J. Rasūlids [Yemen]

626/1229	al-Malik al-Manṣūr ^{C}Umar I	803/1400	al-Malik al-Nāṣir Aḥmad
647/1250	al-Malik al-Muẓaffar Yūsuf I	827/1424	al-Malik al-Manṣūr ^{C}Abdullāh
694/1295	al-Malik al-Ashraf ^{C}Umar II	830/1427	al-Malik al-Ashraf Ismā^{C}īl II
696/1296	al-Malik al-Mu'ayyad Dā'ud	831/1428	al-Malik al-Ẓāhir Yaḥyā
721/1322	al-Malik al-Mujāhid ^{C}Alī	842/1439	al-Malik al-Ashraf Ismā^{C}īl III
764/1363	al-Malik al-Afḍal al-^{C}Abbās	845/1442	al-Malik al-Muẓaffar Yūsuf II
778/1377	al-Malik al-Ashraf Ismā^{C}īl I		

RIVALS

846/1442	al-Malik al-Mufaḍḍal Muḥammad
846/1442	al-Malik al-Nāṣir ^{C}Abdullāh
854/1450	al-Malik al-Mas^{C}ūd
855/1451	al-Malik al-Mu'ayyad

M. Qāsimid Zaydī Imāms [Modern Period]

1000/1592	al-Qāsim al-Manṣūr	1190/1776	ᶜAlī al-Manṣūr
1029/1620	Muḥammad al-Mu'ayyad I	1221/1806	Aḥmad al-Mahdī
1054/1644	Ismāᶜīl al-Mutawakkil	? ?	ᶜAlī al-Manṣūr [2nd reign]
1087/1676	Muḥammad al-Mu'ayyad II	1257/1841	al-Qāsim al-Mahdī
1092/1681	Muḥammad al-Hādī	1261/1845	Muḥammad Yaḥyā
1097/1686	Muḥammad al-Mahdī	1289/1872	Ottoman Occupation
1128/1716	al-Qāsim al-Mutawakkil	1308/1890	Ḥamīd al-Dīn Yaḥyā
1139/1726	al-Ḥusayn al-Manṣūr [1st reign]	1322/1904	Yaḥyā Maḥmūd al-Mutawakkil
1139/1726	Muḥammad al-Hādī al-Majīd	1367/1948	Sayf al-Islām Aḥmad
1140/1728	al-Ḥusayn al-Manṣūr [2nd reign]	1382/1962	Muḥammad Badr
1160/1747	al-ᶜAbbās al-Mahdī		

P. Saᶜūdī Family

1159/1746	Muḥammad b. Saᶜūd	1305/1887	ᶜAbd al-Raḥmān b. Fayṣal [Governor for Rashīdī]
1179/1765	ᶜAbd al-ᶜAzīz I	1308/1891	Rashīdī occupation of Riyāḍh
1218/1803	Saᶜūd b. ᶜAbd al-ᶜAzīz	1319/1902	ᶜAbd al-ᶜAzīz II
1229/1814	ᶜAbdullāh I b. Saᶜūd	1373/1953	Saᶜūd
1233-38/1818-22	Ottoman Occupation	1384/1964	Fayṣal II
1238/1823	Turkī	1395/1975	Khālid
1249/1834	Fayṣal I [1st reign]	1402/1982	Fahd
1253/1837	Khālid b. Saᶜūd		
1257/1841	ᶜAbdullāh II b. Thunayyān		
1259/1843	Fayṣal I [2nd reign]		
1282/1865	ᶜAbdullāh III b. Fayṣal [1st reign]		
1287/1871	Saᶜūd b. Fayṣal		
1291/1874	ᶜAbdullāh III [2nd reign]		

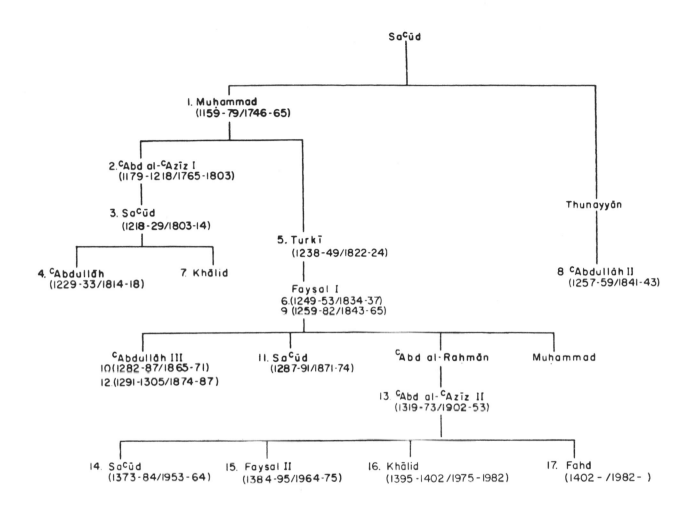

IV. **IRAQ AND SYRIA [Before the Seljuks]**

	Muslim Dates	Christian Dates
*+ A. Ḥamdānids:	317 - 394 A.H.	927 - 1004 A.D.
1. Mosul Branch	317 - 391	927 - 1000
2. Aleppo Branch	333 - 394	945 - 1004
B. Mirdāsids	414 - 472	1023 - 1079
C. ᶜUqaylids	380 - 489	990 - 1096
D. Marwānids	372 - 478	983 - 1085
E. Mazyadids	350 - 545	961 - 1150
F. Inālids	490 - 579	1096 - 1183

A.1. Hamdānids - Mosul Branch

317/929	Nāṣir al-Dawla al-Ḥasan	379/401	Ibrāhīm	] Joint Rulers
358/969	ᶜUddat al-Dawla Abū Taghlib	989/1010	al-Ḥusayn	]

A.2. Hamdānids - Aleppo Branch

333/945	Sayf al-Dawla ᶜAlī I	392/1002	ᶜAlī II
356/967	Saᶜd al-Dawla Sharīf I	394/1004	Sharīf II
381/991	Saᶜīd al-Dawla Saᶜīd		

CAUCASUS [Before the Seljuks]

	Muslim Dates	Christian Dates
A. Sājids	266 - 318 A.H.	879 - 930 A.D.
B. Musāfirids [or Sallarids or Kangarids]	304 - 483	916 - 1090
C. Rawwādids	4th C. - 463	10th C. - 1071
D. Sharwān Shāhs:		
1. First Dynasty	183 - 381	799 - 991
2. Second Dynasty	418 - 455	1027 - 1063
3. Fourth Dynasty	1180 - 1236	1766 - 1821
E. Shaddādids	340 - 571	951 - 1174
F. Dābūyids	40 - 142	660 - 760
G. Bāwandids:	45 - 750	665 - 1349
1. Kā'ūsīya Line	45 - 466	665 - 1074
2. Ispahbadīya Line	466 - 606	1074 - 1210
3. Kinkhwārīya Line	635 - 750	1238 - 1349
H. Bāduspānids	40 - 1006	665 - 1599
I. Zaydī ᶜAlīds of Tabaristan	250 - 316	864 - 928

IRAN [Before the Seljuks]

			Muslim Dates	Christian Dates
*+	A.	Ṭāhirids	205 - 259 A.H.	821 - 873
*	B.	Sāmānids	204 - 395	819 - 1005
*	C.	Ṣaffārids	253 - ca. 900	867 - ca. 1495
	D.	Būyids [Buwayhids]:	320 - 447	932 - 1055
*+		1. Iraq	334 - 447	945 - 1055
*+		2. Fārs and Khūzistān	322 - 454	934 - 1062
*+		3. Kirmān	324 - 440	936 - 1048
*+		4. Jibāl	320 - 366	932 - 977
*+		5. Hamadān and Iṣfahān	366 - 419	977 - 1028
*+		6. Rayy	366 - 420	977 - 1029
		7. ᶜUmān	363 - 388	974 - 998
	E.	Dulafids	210 - 284	825 - 898
	F.	Banijurids	233 - 337	848 - 948
	G.	Qarakhānids [Ĭlek Khāns]	382 - 607	992 - 1211
	H.	Khwārazm Shāhs:		
		1. Afrīghids	? - 385	? - 995
		2. Ma'mūnids	385 - 408	995 - 1017
		3. Governors	408 - 425	1017 - 1034
*		4. Anūshtigin Line	470 - 624	1077 - 1231
	I.	Ziyārids	315 - 483	927 - 1090
	J.	Ḥasanwayhids	348 - 405	959 - 1014
	K.	Ilyāsids	320 - 357	932 - 968
	L.	Kākūyids [Kākwayhids]	398 - 443	1008 - 1051

A. Ṭāhirids

205/821	Ṭāhir I b. al-Husayn		230/845	Ṭāhir II
207/822	Talḥa		248-59/862-73	Muḥammad
213/828	ᶜAbdullāh			

1. Ṭāhir I (Dhū-l-Yamīnayn)
(205-7/821-2)

2. Ṭalḥa
(207-13/822-28)

3. ᶜAbdullāh
(213-30/828-45)

4. Ṭāhir II
(230-48/845-62)

5. Muḥammad
(248-59/862-73)

B. Sāmānids

204/819	Aḥmad I b. Asad b. Sāmān	343/954	al-Amīr al-Mu'ayyad ᶜAbd al-Malik I
250/864	Naṣr I b. Aḥmad		
279/892	Ismāᶜīl I b. Aḥmad	350/961	al-Amīr al-Sadīd Manṣūr I
295/907	Aḥmad II b. Ismāᶜīl	365/976	al-Amīr al-Riḍā Nūḥ II
301/914	al-Amīr al-Saᶜīd Naṣr II	387/997	Manṣūr II
331/943	al-Amīr al-Ḥamīd Nūḥ I	389/999	ᶜAbd al-Malik II
		390-95/1000-05	Ismāᶜīl II al-Muntaṣir

C. Saffārids

253/867	Yaᶜqūb b. Layth al-Ṣaffār	296/908	Layth b. ᶜAlī
265/879	ᶜAmr b. Layth	298/910	Muḥammad b. ᶜAlī
288/901	Ṭāhir b. Muḥammad b. ᶜAmr		

Note: A full list can be found in Bosworth, p. 103.

D.1. Būyids [Buwayhids] in Iraq

334/945	Muᶜizz al-Dawla Aḥmad	403/1012	Sulṭān al-Dawla
356/967	ᶜIzz al-Dawla Bakhtiyār	412/1021	Musharrif al-Dawla Ḥasan
367/978	ᶜAḍud al-Dawla Fanā-Khusraw	416/1025	Jalāl al-Dawla Shīrzīl
372/983	Ṣamṣām al-Dawla Marzubān	435/1044	ᶜImād al-Dīn al-Marzubān
376/987	Sharaf al-Dawla Shīrzīl	440-47/1048-55	al-Malik al-Raḥīm Khusraw-Fīrūz
379/989	Bahā' al-Dawla Fīrūz		

D.2. Būyids in Fārs and Khūzistān

322/932	ᶜImād al-Dawla ᶜAlī	403/1012	Sulṭān al-Dawla
338/949	ᶜAḍud al-Dawla Fanā-Khusraw	412/1021	Musharrif al-Dawla Ḥasan
372/983	Sharaf al-Dawla Shīrzīl	415/1024	ᶜImād al-Dīn Marzubān
380/990	Ṣamṣām al-Dawla Marzubān	440/1048	al-Malik al-Raḥīm Khusraw-Fīrūz
388/998	Bahā' al-Dawla F.rūz	447-54/1055-62	Fūlād-Sutūn [Fārs only]

D.3. Būyids in Kirmān

324/936	Muᶜizz al-Dawla Aḥmad	388/998	Bahā' al-Dawla Fīrūz
338/949	ᶜAḍud al-Dawla Fanā-Khusraw	403/1012	Qawām al-Dawla
372/983	Ṣamṣām al-Dawla Marzubān	419-40/1028-48	ᶜImād al-Dīn Marzubān

---

D.4. Būyids in Jibāl

320/932	ᶜImād al-Dawla ᶜAlī	335-366/947-977	Rukn al-Dawla Ḥasan

---

D.5. <u>Būyids in Hamadān and Isfahān</u>

| 366/977 | Mu'ayyid al-Dawla Būya | 387/997 | Shams al-Dawla |
| 373/983 | Fakhr al-Dawla ^CAlī | 412-c.419/1021-c.28 | Samā' al-Dawla |

D.6. <u>Būyids in Rayy</u>

| 366/977 | Fakhr al-Dawla ^CAlī | 387-420/997-1029 | Majd al-Dawla Rustam |

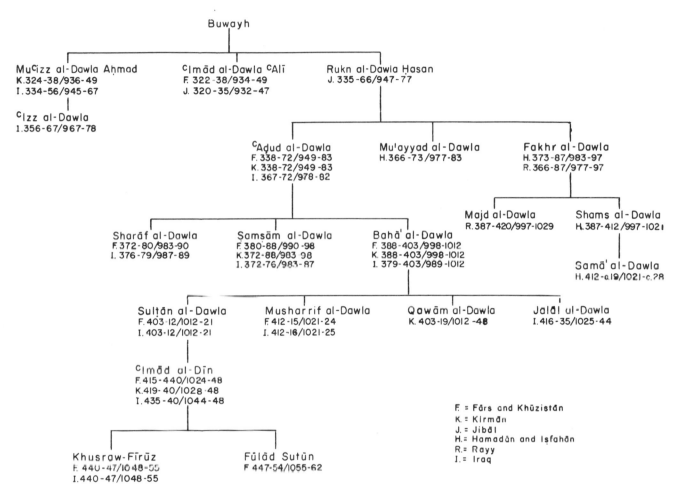

F. = Fārs and Khūzistān
K. = Kirmān
J. = Jibāl
H.= Hamadān and Isfahān
R.= Rayy
I.= Iraq

H.4. <u>Khwārazm Shāhs - Anūshtigin Line</u>

ca.470/ca.1077	Anūshtigin Gharcha'ī	567/1172	^CAlā' al-Dīn Tekish
490/1097	Turkish Governor	567-89/1172-93	Rival Ruler
490/1097	Quṭb al-Dīn Muḥammad	596/1200	^CAlā' al-Dīn Muḥammad
521/1127	^CAlā' al-Dīn Atsīz	617-28/1220-31	Jalāl al-Dīn
551/1156	Īl-Arslān		

SELJUKS AND ATABEGS

		Muslim Dates	Christian Dates
A. Seljuks:		429 - 700 A.H.	1037 - 1300 A.D.
*+	1. Great Seljuks	429 - 552	1037 - 1157
	2. Seljuks of Iraq	511 - 590	1117 - 1194
	3. Seljuks of Syria	471 - 511	1078 - 1117
	4. Seljuks of Kirmān	433 - 583	1041 - 1187
	5. Seljuks of Rum	[See VIII, Asia Minor]	-- --
B. Būrids		497 - 549	1104 - 1154
C. Zangids:			
*+	1. Mosul	521 - 619	1127 - 1222
*+	2. Aleppo	541 - 577	1146 - 1181
	3. Sinjār	566 - 617	1170 - 1220
	4. Jazīra	576 - 648	1180 - 1250
D. Begteginids		539 - 630	1145 - 1233
E. Artuqids:		491 - 811	1098 - 1408
	1. Ḥisn Kayfā Line	491 - 629	1098 - 1232
	2. Mārdin Line	497 - 811	1104 - 1408
F. Suqman Shāhs		493 - 604	1100 - 1207
G. Eldeguzids [or Ildenizids]		531 - 622	1136 - 1225
H. Salghurids		543 - 668	1148 - 1270
I. Faḍlawayhids		448 - 718	1056 - 1318
J. Hazarāspids		550 - 827	1155 - 1424
K. Qutlugh Khāns		619 - 706	1222 - 1306

A.1. Great Seljuks

429/1038	Rukn al-Dunyā wa-1-Dīn Toghril I [Tughril]	487/1094	Rukn al-Dīn Berk-yāruq [Barkiyāruq]
455/1063	ᶜAdud al-Dawla Alp-Arslān	498/1105	Muᶜizz al-Dīn Malik-Shāh II
465/1072	Jalāl al-Dawla Malik Shāh I	498/1105	Ghiyāth al-Dīn Muḥammad I
485/1092	Nāṣir al-Dīn Maḥmūd I	511-52/1118-57	Muᶜizz al-Dīn Sanjar

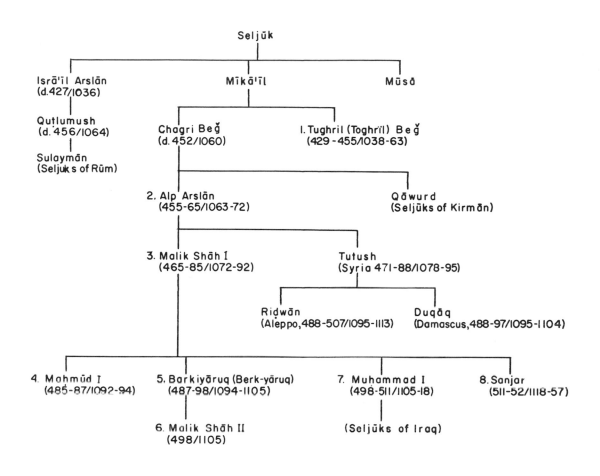

Seljūk

- Isrā'īl Arslān (d.427/1036)
  - Qutlumush (d. 456/1064)
    - Sulaymān (Seljuks of Rūm)
- Mīkā'īl
  - Chaġri Beğ (d. 452/1060)
  - 1. Tughril (Toghrïl) Beğ (429-455/1038-63)
    - 2. Alp Arslān (455-65/1063-72)
    - Qāwurd (Seljūks of Kirmān)
      - 3. Malik Shāh I (465-85/1072-92)
      - Tutush (Syria 471-88/1078-95)
        - Riḍwān (Aleppo, 488-507/1095-1113)
        - Duqāq (Damascus, 488-97/1095-1104)
        - 4. Maḥmūd I (485-87/1092-94)
        - 5. Barkiyāruq (Berk-yāruq) (487-98/1094-1105)
          - 6. Malik Shāh II (498/1105)
        - 7. Muḥammad I (498-511/1105-18)
          - (Seljūks of Iraq)
        - 8. Sanjar (511-52/1118-57)
- Mūsā

C.1. Zangids - Mosul

521/1127	ᶜImād al-Dīn Zangī b. Aq Sonqur	589/1193	Nūr al-Dīn Arslān Shāh I
541/1146	Sayf al-Dīn Ghāzī I	607/1211	ᶜIzz al-Dīn Masᶜūd II
544/1149	Quṭb al-Dīn Mawdūd	615/1218	Nūr al-Dīn Arslān Shāh II
564/1169	Sayf al Dīn Ghāzī II	616-19/1219-??	Nāṣir al-Dīn Maḥmūd
572/1176	ᶜIzz al-Dīn Masᶜūd I		

C.2. Zangids - Aleppo

541/1146	Nūr al-Dīn Maḥmūd b. Zangī	569-77/1174-81	Nūr al-Dīn Ismāᶜīl

1. ᶜImād al-Dīn Zangī
(521-41/1127-46)

2. Sayf al-Dīn Ghāzī I
(541-44/1146-49)

3. Quṭb al-Dīn Mawdūd
(544-64/1149-69)

a. Nūr al-Dīn Maḥmūd
(541-69/1146-74)

b. Nūr al-Dīn Ismāᶜīl
(564-77/1174-81)

4. Sayf al-Dīn Ghāzī II
(564-72/1169-76)

5. ᶜIzz al-Dīn Masᶜūd I
(572-89/1176-93)

6. Nūr al-Dīn Arslān Shāh I
(589-607/1193-1211)

7. ᶜIzz al-Dīn Masᶜūd II
(607-15/1211-18)

8. Nūr al-Dīn Arslān Shāh II
(615-16/1218-19)

9. Nāṣir al-Dīn Maḥmūd
(616-19/1219-22)

ASIA MINOR AND TURKEY

		Muslim Dates	Christian Dates
*	A. Seljuks of Rum	470 - 707 A.H.	1077 - 1307 A.D.
	B. Menqŭchekids	464 - ca. 650	1071 - 1252
	C. Dānishmandids	464 - 573	1071 - 1177
	D. Isfendiyarids	690 - 866	1291 - 1461
	E. Ṣārū Khānids	700 - 813	1300 - 1410
	F. Aydīnids	708 - 829	1308 - 1425
	G. Germiyāndids	699 - 832	1300 - 1429
	H. Ḥamīdids	700 - 826	1239 - 1423
	I. Menteshādids	700 - 829	1300 - 1426
	J. Eretnaids	736 - 782	1335 - 1380
	K. Ramaḍānids	780 - 819	1378 - 1416
	L. Dhū-l-Qadrids	738 - 928	1337 - 1522
	M. Karamānids	654 - 888	1256 - 1483
*+	N. Ottomans	680 - 1342	1281 - 1924
*+	O. Köprülü Vezirs	1066 - 1122	1656 - 1710
*	P. Presidents of Turkey		1923 -

A. Seljuks of Rum

470/1077	Sulaymān b. Quṭlumush
479/1086	Interregnum
485/1092	Qilich Arslān I
500/1107	Malik-Shāh
510/1116	Rukn al-Dīn Mas^cūd I
551/1156	^cIzz al-Dīn Qilich Arslān II
588/1192	Ghiyāth al-Dīn Kay-Khusraw I [1st reign]
592/1196	Rukn al-Dīn Sulaymān II
600/1204	^cIzz al-Dīn Qilich Arslān III
601/1204	Ghiyāth al-Dīn Kay-Khusraw I [2nd reign]
607/1210	^cIzz al-Dīn Kay-Kā'ūs I
616/1219	^cAlā' al-Dīn Kay-Qubādh I
634/1237	Ghiyāth al-Dīn Kay-Khusraw II
644/1246	^cIzz al-Dīn Kay-Kā'ūs II

646/1248	Kay-Kā'ūs II] Jointly
	Rukn al-Dīn Qilich Arslān IV]
647/1249	Kay-Kā'ūs II]
	Qilich Arslān IV ⌉ Jointly
	^cAlā' al-Dīn Kay-Qubādh II]
655/1257	Qilich Arslān IV
663/1265	Ghiyāth al-Dīn Kay-Khusraw III
681/1282	Ghiyāth al-Dīn Mas^cūd II [1st reign]
683/1284	^cAlā' al-Dīn Kay-Qubādh III [1st reign]
683/1284	Mas^cūd II [2nd reign]
692/1293	Kay-Qubādh III [2nd reign]
693/1294	Mas^cūd II [3rd reign]
700/1301	Kay-Qubādh III [3rd reign]
702/1303	Mas^cūd II [4th reign]
704/1305	Kay-Qubādh III [4th reign]
707/1307	Ghiyāth al-Dīn Mas^cūd III

N. The Ottomans

ca.679/1280	Ertuğrul
ca.680/1281	Osmān
724/1324	Orhān
761/1360	Murād I
791/1389	Bāyezīd I
805/1403	Interregnum
816/1413	Mehmet (Mehemmed) I Chelebi
824/1421	Murād II [1st reign]
848/1444	Mehmet (Mehemmed) II Fatih
850/1446	Murād II [2nd reign]
855/1451	Mehmed (Mehemmed) II [2nd reign]
886/1481	Bāyezīd II
918/1512	Selīm I Yavuz
926/1520	Süleymān I Kānūnī
974/1566	Selīm II
982/1574	Murād III
1003/1595	Mehmed (Mehemmed) III
1012/1603	Ahmed I
1026/1617	Muṣṭafā I [1st reign]
1027/1618	Osmān II
1031/1622	Muṣṭafā I [2nd reign]

1032/1623	Mehmed IV
1049/1640	Ibrāhīm
1058/1648	Mehmet IV
1099/1687	Süleymān II
1102/1691	Ahmed II
1106/1695	Muṣṭafā II
1115/1703	Ahmed III
1143/1730	Mahmūd I
1168/1754	Osmān III
1171/1757	Muṣṭafā III
1187/1774	^cAbdülhamīd I
1203/1789	Selīm III
1222/1807	Muṣṭafā IV
1223/1808	Mahmūd II
1255/1839	^cAbdülmecīd I
1277/1861	^cAbdülazīz
1293/1876	Murād V
1293/1876	^cAbdülhamīd II
1327/1909	Mehmed V Reshād
1336/1918	Mehmed VI
1341-42/1922-24	^cAbdülmecīd II [caliph only]

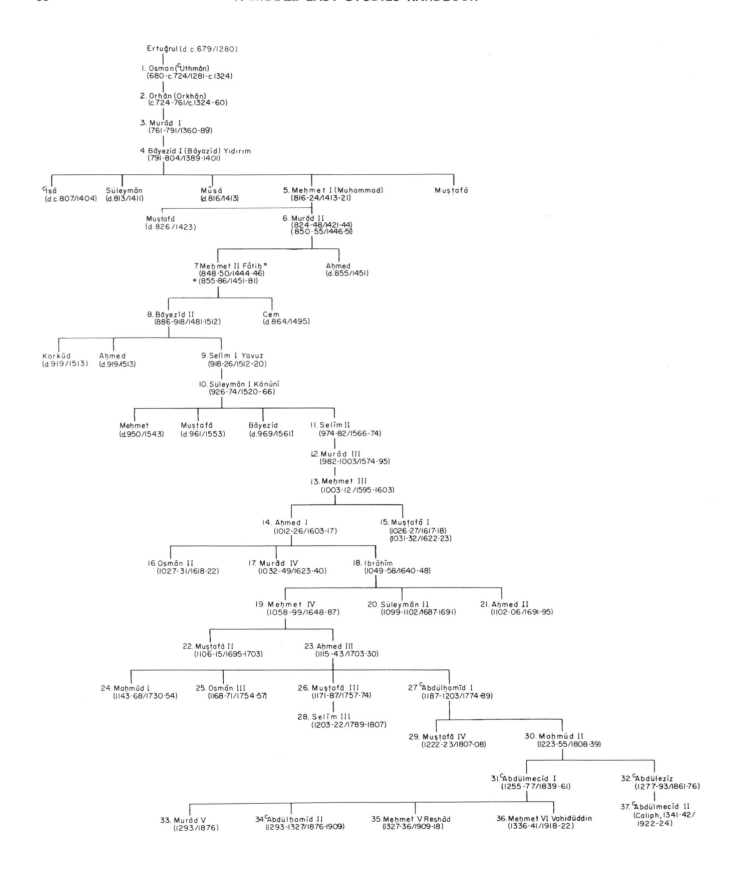

Ertuğrul (d.c.679/1280)

1. Osman (ʿUthmān)
(680-c.724/1281-c.1324)

2. Orhān (Orkhān)
(c.724-761/c.1324-60)

3. Murād I
(761-791/1360-89)

4. Bāyezīd I (Bāyazīd) Yıdırım
(791-804/1389-1401)

ʿIsā   Süleymān   Mūsā   5. Mehmet I (Muhammad)   Muṣṭafā
(d.c.807/1404)   (d.813/1411)   (d.816/1413)   (816-24/1413-21)

Muṣṭafā   6. Murād II
(d.826/1423)   (824-48/1421-44)
                           (850-55/1446-51)

7. Mehmet II Fātiḥ *   Ahmed
(848-50/1444-46)   (d.855/1451)
* (855-86/1451-81)

8. Bāyezīd II   Cem
(886-918/1481-1512)   (d.864/1495)

Korkūd   Ahmed   9. Selīm I Yavuz
(d.919/1513)   (d.919/1513)   (918-26/1512-20)

10. Süleymān I Kānūnī
(926-74/1520-66)

Mehmet   Muṣṭafā   Bāyezīd   11. Selīm II
(d.950/1543)   (d.961/1553)   (d.969/1561)   (974-82/1566-74)

12. Murād III
(982-1003/1574-95)

13. Mehmet III
(1003-12/1595-1603)

14. Ahmed I   15. Muṣṭafā I
(1012-26/1603-17)   (1026-27/1617-18)
                               (1031-32/1622-23)

16. Osmān II   17. Murād IV   18. Ibrāhīm
(1027-31/1618-22)   (1032-49/1623-40)   (1049-58/1640-48)

19. Mehmet IV   20. Süleymān II   21. Ahmed II
(1058-99/1648-87)   (1099-1102/1687-1691)   (1102-06/1691-95)

22. Muṣṭafā II   23. Ahmed III
(1106-15/1695-1703)   (1115-43/1703-30)

24. Mahmūd I   25. Osmān III   26. Muṣṭafā III   27. ʿAbdülhamīd I
(1143-68/1730-54)   (1168-71/1754-57)   (1171-87/1757-74)   (1187-1203/1774-89)

28. Selīm III   29. Muṣṭafā IV   30. Mahmūd II
(1203-22/1789-1807)   (1222-23/1807-08)   (1223-55/1808-39)

31. ʿAbdülmecīd I   32. ʿAbdüleziz
(1255-77/1839-61)   (1277-93/1861-76)

                                                          37. ʿAbdülmecīd II
                                                          (Caliph, 1341-42/
                                                          1922-24)

33. Murād V   34. ʿAbdülhamīd II   35. Mehmet V Reshād   36. Mehmet VI Vahidüddin
(1293/1876)   (1293-1327/1876-1909)   (1327-36/1909-18)   (1336-41/1918-22)

XXIV OTTOMANS (680-1342/1281-1924)

O. <u>Köprülü Vezirs</u>

1066-72/1656-61	Meḥmed Paşa	1101-02/1689-91	Fāẓil Muṣṭafā Paşa
1072-87/1661-76	Fāẓil Aḥmed Paşa	1109-14/1697-1702	Ḥüseyin Paşa
1087-95/1676-83	Kara Muṣṭafā Paşa [by marriage]	1122/1710	Nuᶜmān Paşa

P. <u>Presidents of Turkey</u>

1923	Muṣṭafā Kemal Atatürk	1973	Fahri Korutürk
1938	İsmet İnönü	1980	Ihsan Sabri Çağlayangil [Acting President]
1950	Celal Bayar	1980	Kenan Evren
1961	Cemal Gürsel	1990	Turgut Özal
1966	Cevdet Sunay	1993	Süleyman Demirel

<u>M O N G O L S</u>

		Muslim Dates	Christian Dates
+	A. Great Mongols	603 - 1043 A.H.	1206 - 1634 A.D.
*+	B. Īl-Khānids	654 - 754	1256 - 1353
	C. Golden Horde	621 - 760	1224 - 1359
	D. White Horde	623 - 831	1226 - 1428
	E. Chaghatayids	624 - 771	1227 - 1370
	F. Khāns of Kazan	841 - 959	1438 - 1552
	G. Khāns of Kasimof	854 - 1089	1450 - 1678
	H. Khāns of Crimea	823 - 1197	1420 - 1783

A. <u>Great Mongols</u>

Descendants of Chingiz Khān

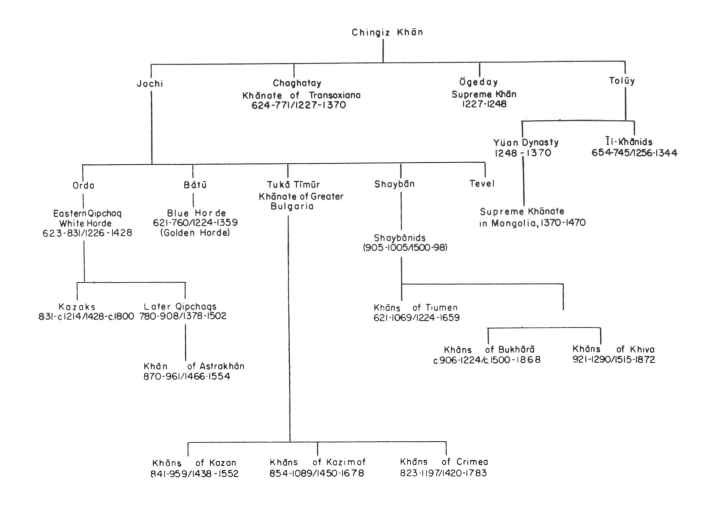

B. <u>Īl-Khānids</u>

654/1256	Hūlegü [Hūlagū]		694/1295	Maḥmūd Ghāzān
663/1265	Abaqa		703/1304	Muḥammad Khudābanda Öljeytü [Ūljaytū]
680/1282	Aḥmad Tegüder [Takūdār]		716/1317	Abū Saᶜīd
683/1284	Arghūn		736/1335	Arpa
690/1291	Gaykhatu		737/1336	Mūsā
694/1295	Baydu		[736-54/1336-53	Period of several rival *khāns*]

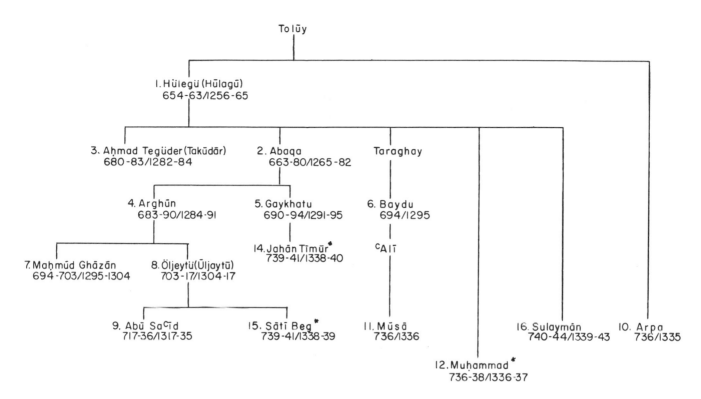

Toluy

1. Hülegü (Hūlagū)
654-63/1256-65

3. Aḥmad Tegüder (Takūdār)   2. Abaqa   Taraghay
680-83/1282-84   663-80/1265-82

4. Arghūn   5. Gaykhatu   6. Baydu
683-90/1284-91   690-94/1291-95   694/1295

                   14. Jahān Tīmūr*   ᶜAlī
                   739-41/1338-40

7. Maḥmūd Ghāzān   8. Öljeytü (Ūljaytū)
694-703/1295-1304 703-17/1304-17

9. Abū Saᶜīd   15. Sātī Beg*   11. Mūsā   16. Sulaymān   10. Arpa
717-36/1317-35   739-41/1338-39   736/1336   740-44/1339-43   736/1335

                                         12. Muḥammad*
                                         736-38/1336-37

13. Tughiā Tīmūr* (738-52/1337-51)

* Nominated by other powers.

X.   IRAN [After the Mongols]

		Muslim Dates	Christian Dates
	A. Jalāyirids	736 - 835 A.H.	1336 - 1432 A.D.
	B. Muzaffarids	713 - 795	1314 - 1393
	C. Īnjūids	703 - 758	1303 - 1357
	D. Sarbadārids	758 - 781	1357 - 1379
	E. Karts	643 - 791	1245 - 1389
	F. Qara Qoyunlu	782 - 873	1380 - 1468
	G. Aq Qoyunlu	780 - 914	1378 - 1508
*+	H. Ṣafavids	907 - 1145	1501 - 1732
*	I. Afshārids	1148 - 1210	1736 - 1795
*	J. Zands	1163 - 1209	1750 - 1794
*+	K. Qājārs	1193 - 1342	1779 - 1924
*	L. Pahlavi	1344 - 1400	1925 - 1979
*	M. Presidents of Islamic Republic of Iran	1400 -	1979 -

H. Safavids

907/1501	Ismāᶜīl I	1038/1629	Ṣafī I	1145/1732	ᶜAbbās III
930/1524	Ṭahmāsp I	1052/1642	ᶜAbbās II	1163/1749	Sulaymān II
984/1576	Ismāᶜīl II	1077/1666	Sulaymān I [Ṣafī II]	1163/1750	Ismāᶜīl III
985/1578	Muḥammad Khudabānda	1105/1694	Ḥusayn I	1166/1753	Ḥusayn II
996/1588	ᶜAbbās I	1135/1722	Ṭahmāsp II	1200/1786	Muḥammad

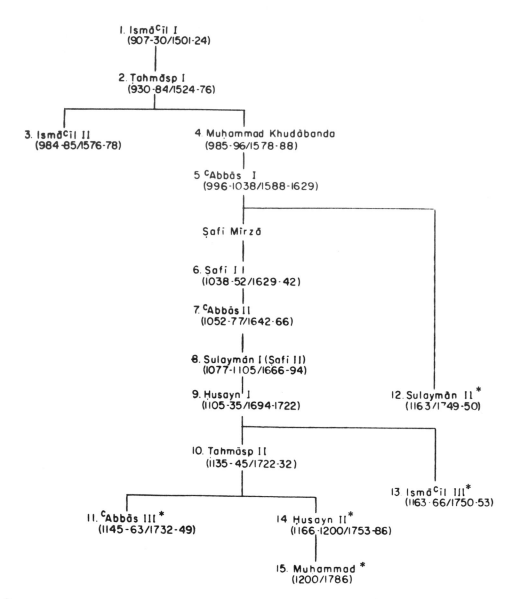

1. Ismāᶜīl I
(907-30/1501-24)

2. Ṭahmāsp I
(930-84/1524-76)

3. Ismāᶜīl II
(984-85/1576-78)

4. Muḥammad Khudābanda
(985-96/1578-88)

5. ᶜAbbās I
(996-1038/1588-1629)

Ṣafī Mīrzā

6. Ṣafī I
(1038-52/1629-42)

7. ᶜAbbās II
(1052-77/1642-66)

8. Sulaymān I (Ṣafī II)
(1077-1105/1666-94)

9. Ḥusayn I
(1105-35/1694-1722)

12. Sulaymān II *
(1163/1749-50)

10. Ṭahmāsp II
(1135-45/1722-32)

13. Ismāᶜīl III *
(1163-66/1750-53)

11. ᶜAbbās III *
(1145-63/1732-49)

14 Ḥusayn II *
(1166-1200/1753-86)

15. Muḥammad *
(1200/1786)

*Nominal rulers

I. Afshārids

1148/1736	Nādir Shāh [Ṭahmāsp Qulī Khān]	1161/1748	Ibrāhīm
1160/1747	ᶜĀdil Shāh [ᶜAlī Qulī Khān]	1161-1210/1748-95	Shāh Rukh [in Khurāsān]

J. The Zands

1163/1750	Muḥammad Karīm Khān	1193-99/1779-85	ᶜAlī Murād [in Iṣfahān]
1193/1779	Abū-l-Fatḥ]	1199/1785	Jaᶜfar
	Muḥammad ᶜAlī] Joint Rulers	1203-09/1789-94	Luṭf ᶜAlī
1193-95/1779-81	Ṣādiq [in Shīrāz]		

K. The Qājārs

1193/1779	Āghā Muḥammad	1313/1896	Muẓaffar al-Dīn
1212/1797	Fatḥ ᶜAlī Shāh	1324/1907	Muḥammad ᶜAlī
1250/1834	Muḥammad	1327-42/1909-24	Aḥmad
1264/1848	Nāṣir al-Dīn		

Fatḥ ᶜAlī Khān
(d. 1163/1750)

Muhammad Ḥasan Khān
(d. 1163/1750)

1. Āghā Muḥammad
(1193-1212/1779-97)

Ḥusayn Qulī Khān
(d. 1193/1779)

2. Fatḥ ᶜAlī Shāh
(1212-50/1797-1834)

ᶜAbbās Mirza

3. Muḥammad
(1250-64/1834-48)

4. Nāṣir al-Dīn
(1264-1313/1848-96)

5. Muẓaffar al-Din
(1313-24/1896-1907)

6. Muḥammad ᶜAlī
(1324-27/1907-09)

7. Aḥmad
(1327-42/1909-24)

L. Pahlavi Dynasty

1925 - 1941	Reza Shāh	1941 - 1979	Mohammed Reza Shāh

M. Presidents of Islamic Republic of Iran

1980   Abū-l-Ḥasan Banī-Sadr
1981   Muḥammad ^CAlī Rajā'i

        Alī Khamān^Ci

TRANSOXIANA AND AFGHANISTAN

		Muslim Dates	Christian Dates
*	A. Tīmūrids	771 - 912 A.H.	1370 - 1506 A.D.
	B. Shaybānids	905 - 1007	1500 - 1598
	C. Jānids	1009 - 1199	1559 - 1785
	D. Mangits	1170 - 1339	1757 - 1920
	E. Khāns of Khiva	921 - 1290	1515 - 1872
*+	F. Ghaznavids	366 - 582	977 - 1186
	G. Ghūrids	390 - 612	1000 - 1215

A. Tīmūrids

771/1370	Tīmūr [Temur]
807/1405	Khalīl [until 812/1409]
807/1405	Shāh Rukh
850/1447	Ulugh Beg
853/1449	^CAbd al-Laṭīf

854/1450	^CAbdullāh
855/1451	Abū Sa^Cīd
873/1469	Aḥmad
899-906/1494-1500	Maḥmūd b. Abī Sa^Cīd

F. Ghaznavids

366/977	Nāṣir al-Dawla Sebüktigīn
387/997	Ismā^Cīl
388/998	Maḥmūd
421/1030	Muḥammad [1st reign]
421/1031	Mas^Cūd I
432/1041	Muḥammad [2nd reign]
432/1041	Shihāb al-Dawla Mawdūd
441/1050	Mas^Cūd II
441/1050	^CAlī
441/1050	^CAbd al-Rashīd

444/1053	Qawām al-Dawla Toghril [Usurper]
444/1053	Farrukhzād
451/1059	Ibrāhīm
492/1099	Mas^Cūd III
508/1114	Shīrzād
509/1115	Arslaň Shāh
512/1118	Bahrām Shāh
547/1152	Khusraw Shāh
555-582/1160-86	Khusraw Malik

1. Sebüktigīn
(366-87/977-97)

2. Ismāᶜīl
(387-88/997-98)

3. Maḥmūd
(388-421/998-1030)

4. Muhammad
(421/1030 and
432/1041)

5. Masᶜūd I
(421-32/1030-41)

9. ᶜAbd al-Rashīd
(441-44/1050-53)

6. Mawdūd
(432-41/1041-50)

8. ᶜAlī
(441/1050)

11. Farrukhzād
(444-51/1053-59)

12. Ibrāhim
(451-92/1059-99)

7. Masᶜūd II
(441/1050)

13. Masᶜūd III
(492-508/1099-1114)

14. Shīrzād
(508-09/1114-15)

15. Arslān Shāh
(509-12/1115-1118)

16. Bahrām Shāh
(512-47/1118-52)

17. Khusraw Shāh
(547-55/1152-60)

10. Qawām al-Dawla Toghrïl, usurper (444/1053)

18. Khusraw Malik
(555-82/1160-86)

IRAQ AND GREATER SYRIA [Since World War I]

		Christian Dates
*	A. British High Commissioners for Palestine	1920 - 1948 A.D.
	B. French High Commissioners and Delegate Generals:	
*	1. Lebanon	1919 - 1926
*	2. Syria	1923 - 1946
	C. Ḥāshimites:	
*+	1. Hejaz	1908 - 1925
*+	2. Jordan/Transjordan	1921 -
*+	3. Iraq	1921 - 1958
*	D. Presidents of Lebanon	1926 -
*	E. Rulers of Syria	1945 -
*	F. Presidents of Israel	1948 -
*	G. Prime Ministers of Israel	1949 -
*	H. Rulers of Iraq	1958 -

A. Palestine - British High Commissioners

1920	Sir Herbert Samuel	1937	Sir Harold MacMichael
1925	Lord Plumer	1944	Lord Gort
1928	Sir John Chancellor	1945-48	Sir Alan Cunningham
1931	Sir Arthur Wauchope		

B.1. Lebanon - French High Commissioners and Delegate Generals

| 1919 | Gen. Henri Gouraud | 1926 | Henri Ponsot |

B.2. Syria - French High Commissioners and Delegate Generals

1923	Gen. Maxime Weygand	1940	Gen. Henri-Fernand Dentz
1925	Gen. Maurice Sarrail	1941	Gen. Georges Catroux
1925	Henri de Jouvenal	1943	Yves Chataigneau
1933	Damien de Martel	1943	Jean Helleu
1938	Gabriel Puaux	1944-46	Gen. Paul Emile Beynet

C.1. Hāshimites - Hejaz

| 1908 | Ḥusayn [Amīr] | 1924-25 | ᶜAlī |
| 1916 | Ḥusayn [King] | | |

C.2. Hāshimites - Transjordan/Jordan

1921	ᶜAbdallāh [Amīr]	1952	Ḥusayn
1946	ᶜAbdallāh [King]		
1951	Ṭalāl		

C.3. Hāshimites - Iraq

| 1921 | Fayṣal I | 1939-58 | Fayṣal II |
| 1933 | Ghāzī | | |

Husayn (d.1931)
(1908-16 - Amīr of Hejaz)
(1916-24 -King)

ᶜAli (d.1935)
(1924-25 - King of Hejaz)

ᶜAbd al-Ilāh (d.1958)
(1939-53-Regent of Iraq)

ᶜAbdullāh
(1921-46·Transjordan Amir)
(1946-51 - King)

Faysal I
(1919-20-Syria)
(1921-33-Iraq)

Zayd

Talāl
(1951-52-Jordan)

Nā'if

Ghāzi
(1933-39·Iraq)

Husayn
(1952- , Jordan)

Faysal II
(1939-58·Iraq)

D. Presidents of Lebanon

1926	Sharl Dabbās [Charles Dabbas]
1934	Ḥabīb al-Saᶜd [Habib Sa'd]
1936	Imīl Iddi [Emile Edde]
1941	Alfred Naqqāsh [Alfred Naccache]
1943	ᶜAyyūb Thābit [Eyub Tabet]
1943	Batru Trād [Petro Trad]
1943	Bishārah al-Khūrī [Bishara Khuri]
1952	Kamīl Shimᶜūn [Camille Chamoun]
1958	Fu'ād Shihāb [Gen. Fouad Chehab]

1964	Sharl Ḥilū [Charles Helou]
1970	Sulaymān Franjīyah [Suleiman Franjieh]
1976	Ilyās Sarkīs [Elias Sarkis]
1982	Amīn al-Jumayyil [Amin Gemayel]

E. Rulers of Syria

1945	Shukrī al-Quwatlī
1949	Ḥusnī Zaᶜīm
1949	Sāmī al-Ḥinnāwī
1949	Adīb Shīshaklī
1954	Akram al-Hawrānī] ᶜAbd al-Ḥamīd al-Sarrāj] Diumvirate
1958	United Arab Republic

1961	Nazīm al-Qudsī [President]
1963	Amīn al-Ḥāfiz
1966	Ṣalaḥ Jadīd
1970	Ḥāfiz al-Asad

F. Presidents of Israel

1948	Chaim Weizmann
1952	Itzhak Ben-Zvi
1963	Zalman Shazar
1973	Ephraim Katzir
1978	Itzhak Navon

1983	Chaim Herzog

G. <u>Prime Ministers of Israel</u>

1949	David Ben-Gurion	1983	Yitzhak Shamir
1953	Moshe Sharett		
1955	David Ben-Gurion		
1963	Levi Eshkol [d. February 26, 1969]		
1969	Golda Meir		
1974	Yitzhak Rabin		
1977	Menachem Begin		

————————————————

H. <u>Rulers of Iraq</u>

1958	^CAbd al-Ḥamīd Qāsim	1979	Ṣaddām Ḥusayn al-Takrītī
1963	^CAbd al-Ṣalām ^CĀrif		
1966	^CAbd al-Raḥmān ^CĀrif		
1968	Aḥmad Ḥasan al-Bakr		

————————————————

V. Supplementary Charts

Major Ṣūfī Silsila
Major Arab Tribes: Skeleton Outline
Time Chart, 600-1800 A.D.
Semitic (Afro-Asiatic) Family of Languages
Indo-European and Altaic Families of Languages

MAJOR ṢŪFĪ SILSILA

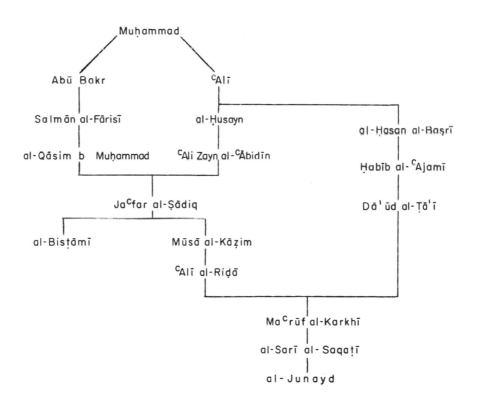

MAJOR ARAB TRIBES: SKELETON OUTLINE

C.   TIME CHART, 600 to 1800 A.D.

SEMITIC [AFRO-ASIATIC] FAMILY OF LANGUAGES

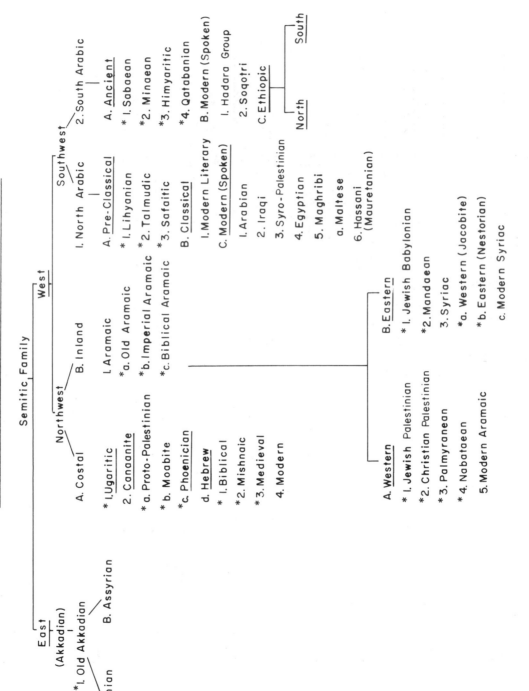

Semitic Family

East (Akkadian)

*A. Babylonian

*I. Old Akkadian

B. Assyrian

West

Northwest

A. Costal

*I. Ugaritic
2. Canaanite
*a. Proto-Palestinian
*b. Moabite
*c. Phoenician
d. Hebrew
    *I. Biblical
    *2. Mishnaic
    *3. Medieval
    4. Modern

B. Inland

I. Aramaic
*a. Old Aramaic
*b. Imperial Aramaic
*c. Biblical Aramaic

A. Western
*I. Jewish Palestinian
*2. Christian Palestinian
*3. Palmyranean
*4. Nabataean
5. Modern Aramaic

B. Eastern
*I. Jewish Babylonian
*2. Mandaean
3. Syriac
    *a. Western (Jacobite)
    *b. Eastern (Nestorian)
    c. Modern Syriac

Southwest

I. North Arabic

A. Pre-Classical
*I. Lihyanian
*2. Talmudic
*3. Safaitic
B. Classical
    I. Modern Literary
C. Modern (Spoken)
    I. Arabian
    2. Iraqi
    3. Syro-Palestinian
    4. Egyptian
    5. Maghribi
        a. Maltese
    6. Hassani (Mauretanian)

2. South Arabic

A. Ancient
*I. Sabaean
*2. Minaean
*3. Himyaritic
*4. Qatabanian
B. Modern (Spoken)
    I. Hadara Group
    2. Soqotri
C. Ethiopic

North   South

*indicates that language or dialect is extinct

INDO-EUROPEAN and ALTAIC FAMILIES OF LANGUAGES

THE INDO-EUROPEAN FAMILY

Indo-Iranian

Iranian

Armenian	Indic	Old Iranian	Middle Iranian
*Classical	*Sanskrit	*Old Persian	*Khotanese
*Cilician	*Prakrit	*Medean	*Soghdian
Modern	Modern	*Avestan	*Middle Parthian
Eastern Western	Hindi		*Middle Persian
	Urdu		*Pahlavi
	etc.		

New Iranian

New Persian	Pashtu
Central	Kurdish
Tajik	Baluchi
Judeo-Persian	etc.

*languages no longer spoken

ALTAIC FAMILY

Turkic	Mongolic		Tungusic
	Buryat	Mongol	Tungus Manchurian
			Korean?

Chuvash	Northwest	Southwest	Southeast	Northeast
Bashkir	Kirghiz	Turkmen	Uigur	Yakut
Tatars	Kipchak	Azeri	Karakalpak	
Karay	Ozbek	Osmanli	Kazakh	
Krimchak		Turkish		

VI. Chronology

The selecting of items for this chonological list is based upon the author's teaching and research experiences. For example, some of the previously listed dynasties, rulers and administrators are listed, but not all of them. In most cases, there is general agreement among scholars as to when events took place, except for incidents during the first three decades of Islam. The foundation dates for the city of al-Kūfa are given in the medieval Arabic sources as A.H. 15, 16, 17 and 18, or any one of four years between 636 and 640 A.D. I have chosen 637. The few other cases of disagreement represent one-year variations between sources.

The most detailed chronology for the period to *circa* 1800 is by Marshall G.S. Hodgson. *The Venture of Islam*, 3 vols. (Chicago: University of Chicago Press, 1974), in his numerous tables. For events since 1947, *MEJ* includes a chronology at the end of each quarterly volume, and they are extremely valuable. Two new annuals are also very helpful:

- Colin Legum, ed., *Middle East Contemporary Survey* (New York: Holmes and Meier), with the first volume covering October 1976 to October 1977.

- David H. Partington, ed., *The Middle East Annual* (Boston: G.K. Hall & Co.), with Volume 1 covering 1981.

There are also various standard references for current events or annual surveys which can be used.

570	Traditional date for birth of Muḥammad.
602	End of Lakhmid dynasty at Ḥīra.
610	Muḥammad received first revelation.
615	Emigration of some Muslims from Mecca to Abyssinia.
622	*Hijra*: Beginning of Muslim calendar.
	Sept. 24: Muḥammad's arrival at Yathrib [Medina/Madīna].
624	Muḥammad's victory at Badr.
625	Muḥammad's temporary defeat at Uḥud.
627	Battle of the Khandaq [Trench] at Medina. Meccans repulsed.
628	Agreement at al-Ḥudaybīyah between Muḥammad and Meccans.
629	Pilgrimage to Mecca.
630	Mecca under Muslim rule.
630-631	"Year of Delegations" of Arab tribal leaders to Muḥammad.
632	March 16 [18 Dhū-1-Ḥijja A.H. 10]: Ghadīr Khumm where, according to Shīᶜite tradition, Muḥammad appointed ᶜAlī his successor.
632	June 8: Death of Muḥammad.
632-634	Reign of Caliph Abū Bakr.
633	End of al-Ridda Wars. Defeat of Musaylima by Khālid b. al-Walīd.
634	Defeat of Byzantines at Ajnadayn.
	Aug.: Death of Abū Bakr.
634-644	Reign of Caliph ᶜUmar.
635	Occupation of Damascus by Khālid b. al-Walīd.
	Expulsion by ᶜUmar of Jews from Khaybar and Christians from Najrān.
636	Defeat of Sassanians at Qādisīya.
637	Defeat of Byzantines at Yarmūk.
	Muslim conquest of Ctesiphon, Sassanian capital.
	Kufa [al-Kūfa] and Basra [al-Baṣra] established as garrison bases [*amṣār*].

638	Muslim conquest of Jerusalem.
640	Jan.: ^CAmr b. al-^CĀṣ entered Egypt.
641	^CAmr b. al-^CĀṣ captured Babylon.
	Fusṭāṭ founded.
	Defeat of Sassanians at Nihawend and fall of Persia.
644	Nov.: Murder of ^CUmar by a non-Muslim slave.
644-656	Reign of Caliph ^CUthmān.
646	Final capture of Alexandria, previously held from 642-645.
649	Conquest of Cyprus by Mu^Cāwiya, Governor of Syria.
651	Yazdigird III, last Sassanian ruler, murdered at Merv.
656	June: Assassination of ^CUthmān by Muslims.
	Dec. 9: Battle of the Camel near Basra; ^CAlī defeated al-Zubayr, Ṭalḥa and ^CĀ'isha.
656-661	Reign of Caliph ^CAlī.
	First civil war.
c.657	Battle of Ṣiffīn between ^CAlī and Mu^Cāwiya.
c.659	Arbitration at Adhruh.
	Battle between ^CAlī and Kharijites at Nahrawān Canal.
661	Jan. 24: ^CAlī murdered by a Kharijite.
	Ḥasan b. ^CAlī renounced claim to caliphate.
661-680	Reign of Caliph Mu^Cāwiya I.
661-750	Umayyad Dynasty.
662-675	Ziyād ibn Abīhi, Governor of Basra; then of Kufa as well.
667	Arabs cross Amū Darya [Oxus].
670	Establishment of Qayrawān.
	^CUqba b. Nāfi^C [d. 683] active in North Africa.
674-679	Siege of Constantinople failed.
680	Oct. 10 [10th Muḥarram A.H. 61]: Ḥusayn b. ^CAlī martyred at Karbalā'.
680-683	Reign of Caliph Yazīd I.
683-692	*Fitnah* of Ibn al-Zubayr [2nd civil war].
683-684	Reign of Caliph Mu^Cāwiya II.
684-685	Reign of Caliph Marwān I.

684	July: Battle of Marj Rāhiṭ.
	Victory of Kalb over Qays.
685-687	Revolt of Mukhtār at al-Kūfa.
685-705	Reign of Caliph ^CAbd al-Malik.
692	al-Ḥajjāj b. Yūsuf ended *fitnah* of Ibn al-Zubayr; occupied Mecca.
694-714	al-Ḥajjāj b. Yūsuf, Governor of Iraq.
696	Introduction of all-Arabic coinage.
705-715	Reign of Caliph Walīd I.
705	Umayyad mosque of Damascus built.
c.705	Wāsiṭ founded a garrison city.
711	Ṭāriq, subordinate of Mūsā b. Nuṣayr, invaded Spain.
711-713	Conquest of Sind and Transoxiana.
714	Death of al-Ḥajjāj.
717-718	Siege of Constantinople under Maslama failed.
717	First Muslim expedition across Pyrenees.
717-720	Reign of Caliph ^CUmar II.
720-724	Reign of Caliph Yazīd II.
720-759	Occupation of Narbonne.
724-743	Reign of Caliph Hishām.
728	Death of mystic, al-Ḥasan al-Baṣrī.
732	Battle of Tours [Poitiers].
	Charles Martel defeated Muslims.
739-742	Anti-Arab Berber revolt in North Africa.
740	Failure of Shī^Cite revolt.
	Death of Zayd.
745-750	Reign of Caliph Marwān II.
747	June: ^CAbbāsid revolt begun by Abū Muslim near Merv.
	Third civil war.
749	Sept.: ^CAbbāsid troops took Kufa.
	Nov.: Abū-l-^CAbbās [posthumously called al-Saffāḥ] proclaimed caliph at Kufa.
750	Feb.: Marwān defeated at Battle of Greater Zāb.
	June: Massacre of most Umayyad family members by ^CAbbāsids.
750-1258	^CAbbāsid dynasty.
750-754	Reign of Caliph Abū-l-^CAbbās al-Saffāḥ.
754-775	Reign of Caliph Abū Ja^Cfar al-Manṣūr.
756-1031	Umayyad dynasty of Spain.

754	Assassination of Abū Muslim by order of al-Manṣūr.
755-788	ᶜAbd al-Raḥmān I in Cordoba.
757	Death of translator and author of Arabic prose, Ibn al-Muqaffaᶜ.
762	Founding of Baghdad [Madīnat al-Salām]. Unsuccessful Shīᶜite revolt at Medina by Muḥammad b. ᶜAbdullāh, "The Pure Soul."
763	Death of Shīᶜite, Ibrāhīm b. ᶜAbdullāh.
765	Death of Jaᶜfar al-Ṣādiq, 6th Shīᶜite Imām.
767	Death of jurisconsult, Abū Ḥanīfa. Death of Ibn Isḥāq, biographer of Muḥammad.
775-785	Reign of Caliph al-Mahdī.
785-786	Reign of Caliph al-Hādī.
786-809	Reign of Caliph Hārūn al-Rashīd.
792	al-Amīn designated successor to Hārūn al-Rashīd.
795	Death of jurisconsult, Mālik b. Anas.
798	Death of jurisconsult, Abū Yūsuf, of the Hanafite *madhhab*.
799	al-Ma'mūn designated 2nd successor to Hārūn al-Rashīd.
800-909	Aghlabid dynasty of North Africa.
801	Death of female mystic, Rābiᶜa.
803	Fall of Barmakid family.
805	Death of jurisconsult, al-Shaybānī of the Hanafite *madhhab*.
806	Major Muslim attack against Byzantium.
809-813	Reign of Caliph al-Amīn. Fourth civil war.
812	Siege of Baghdad by Ṭāhir.
813-833	Reign of Caliph al-Ma'mūn.
816-838	Revolt of Babak, primarily in Azerbaijan.
817	al-Ma'mūn designated ᶜAlī al-Riḍā [d. 818] as successor.
819	al-Ma'mūn entered Baghdad.
820	Death of jurisconsult, al-Shāfiᶜī.
821-873	Ṭāhirid dynasty of Khurāsān.
827	al-Ma'mūn established Muᶜtazilite doctrines as "orthodoxy."
829-831	Revolt of Copts in Egypt.
833-842	Reign of Caliph al-Muᶜtaṣim.

836-889	Samarra ᶜAbbāsid capital.
842-847	Reign of Caliph al-Wāthiq.
847-861	Reign of Caliph al-Mutawakkil.
855	Death of jurisconsult, Aḥmad b. Ḥanbal.
861-908	Most active period of Ṣaffārid dynasty, led by Yaᶜqub al-Ṣaffār [d. 879].
864	Zaydī Shīᶜite dynasty established in Daylam.
868	Death of writer, al-Jāḥiz.
868-905	Ṭūlūnid dynasty of Egypt founded by Aḥmad b. Ṭūlūn [808-884].
869-892	Reign of Caliph al-Muᶜtamid, regent. al-Muwaffaq took charge of ᶜAbbāsid army.
869-883	Zanj revolt.
870	Conquest of Malta. Death of *hadīth* collector, al-Bukhārī.
871	Zanj sacked Basra.
873	Death of philosopher, al-Kindī. Death of translator, Ḥunayn b. Isḥāq. Disappearance of 12th Shīᶜite Imām.
873-940	Lesser or Little Occulation [Ghaybah] for Ithnā ᶜAsharī.
874-999	Sāmānid dynasty of Transoxiana.
877	Aḥmad b. Ṭūlūn began building mosque in al-Qaṭāᶜi.
880s	Rise of Qarmatians.
883	Death of jurisconsult, Dāwūd b. Khalaf of the Zāhirī *madhhab*.
886	Peace agreement between Ṭūlūnid Khumārawayh and Caliph al-Muᶜtamid.
890-1008	Major line of Ḥamdānid dynasty of Iraq and Syria.
892	Death of historian, Aḥmad al-Balādhurī.
901	Establishment of Shīᶜite Zaydī state in Yemen.
902-908	Reign of Caliph al-Muktafī.
908	Dec. 17: One-day caliphate of Ibn al-Muᶜtazz. Revolt in name of Fāṭimid dynasty in North Africa.
909-1171	Fāṭimid dynasty.
910	Death of mystic, al-Junayd.
922	Death of mystic, al-Ḥallāj.

923	Death of historian, al-Ṭabarī.
925	Death of physician, al-Rāzī.
928	Qarmatians stole Black Stone from Ka^cba; held it until 951.
929	^CAbd al-Raḥmān III [912-961] of Umayyads of Spain took title of "caliph."
932-1062	Būyids of Iraq and Iran.
935-969	Ikhshīdid dynasty of Egypt founded by Muḥammad b. Ṭughj.
935	Death of theologian, al-Ash^carī.
936	Ibn Rā'iq became *amīr al-umarā'*.
940	Beginning of Greater Occulation [Ghaybah] for Ithnā ^cAsharī.
944	Peace agreement between Muḥammad b. Ṭughj al-Ikhshīd and Caliph al-Muttaqī.
945-1055	Būyids occupied Baghdad.
950	Death of philosopher, al-Fārābī.
953-975	Reign of al-Mu^cizz, Fāṭimid caliph.
956	Death of historian, al-Mas^cūdī.
962-1186	Ghaznavid dynasty.
962	Alptegīn in Ghazna.
965	Death of poet, al-Mutanabbī.
966-968	Kāfūr ruled Egypt.
969	Jawhar conquered Egypt for Fāṭimids and founded Cairo.
973	al-Azhar was founded.
975-996	Reign of al-^CAzīz, Fāṭimid caliph.
996-1021	Reign of al-Ḥākim, Fāṭimid caliph.
998-1030	Maḥmūd of Ghazna.
1020	Death of poet Firdawsī, author of "Shahnāma."
1030	Death of historian, Miskawayh.
1036-1094	Reign of al-Mustanṣir, Fāṭimid caliph.
1037	Death of philosopher, Ibn Sīnā [Avicenna].
1039	Death of optician, Ibn al-Haytham.
1048	Death of savant, al-Bīrūnī.
1055-1063	Ṭughril Beg entered Baghdad as head of Seljuks.
1058	Death of political theorist, al-Māwardī. Death of poet, Abū-l-^CAlā al-Ma^carrī.
1059	Shī^cite revolt in Iraq, led by al-Basāsīrī.

1063-1072	Reign of Alp Arslān, Seljuk sultan.
1064	Death of philosopher, Ibn Ḥazm.
1065	Establishment of Niẓāmiyyah *madrasa* in Baghdad.
1071	Aug. 26: Battle of Manzikert [Malazgirt] and Byzantine defeat.
1072-1092	Reign of Malik Shāh, Seljuk sultan.
1075	Seljuks of Rūm made Iznik [Nicaea] their capital.
1090	Ḥasan-i Ṣabbāh seized Alamut fortress.
1092	Niẓām al-Mulk murdered by Assassins.
1095	Nov.: Pope Urban at Clermont called for First Crusade.
1097	First Crusade at Constantinople; then took Iznik. Konya became capital of Seljuks of Rūm.
1098	Crusaders captured Antioch.
1099	July 15: Jerusalem conquered by Crusaders.
1100	Baldwin became King of Jerusalem.
1111	Death of philosopher and mystic, al-Ghazzālī.
1118-1157	Reign of Sanjar, Seljuk sultan.
1123	Death of poet and astronomer, ^CUmar Khayyām.
1124	Death of Ḥasan-i Ṣabbāh, leader of Assassins.
1144	Zangī [1127-1146] captured Edessa [Urfa] from Crusaders.
1147	Second Crusade, led by Conrad II and Louis VII.
1148-1215	Ghūrid dynasty of Afghanistan.
1154	Nūr al-Dīn [1146-1174] captured Damascus.
1166	Death of *ṣūfī*, ^CAbd al-Qādir Gīlānī.
1169-1193	Ṣalāḥ al-Dīn [Saladin] controlled Egypt.
1171-1250	Ayyūbid dynasty in Egypt.
1171	Ṣalāḥ al-Dīn ended Fāṭimid dynasty and established Ayyūbid dynasty.
1176	Sept.: Kilij Arslān defeated Byzantine forces at Myriokephalon.
1180-1225	Reign of al-Nāṣir, ^CAbbāsid caliph.
1187	July 4: Ṣalāḥ al-Dīn victorious over Crusaders at Battle of Ḥaṭṭīn.

1189-1192	Third Crusade, led by Frederick Barbarossa, Philip Augustus and Richard I.
1198	Death of philosopher, Ibn Rushd [Averroës].
c.1200	Death of Persian writer, ᶜAṭṭār.
1200-1218	Reign of al-Malik al-ᶜĀdil, Ayyūbid sultan.
1203	Death of Persian poet, Niẓami.
1204-1261	Fourth Crusade and Latin occupation of Constantinople.
1206	Temuchin took title of Chingiz Khān.
1218	Fifth Crusade landed at Damietta.
1218-1238	Reign of al-Malik al-Kāmil, Ayyūbid sultan of Egypt.
1220	Khwarazm Shāhs defeated by Chingiz Khān.
1220-1231	Reign of Khwarazm Shāh Jalāl al-Dīn.
1227	Death of Ghengis Khān.
1229	Death of geographer, Yāqūt.
	Peace treaty between Sixth Crusade, led by Frederick II, and al-Malik al-Kāmil.
1234	Death of historian, Ibn al-Athīr.
1235	Death of ṣūfī poet, Ibn al-Fārid.
1238-1492	Naṣrid dynasty of Granada.
1240	Death of philosopher, Ibn ᶜArabī.
1242-1258	Reign of al-Mustaᶜṣim, last ᶜAbbāsid caliph of Baghdad.
1243	Mongols defeated Seljuks of Rūm at Kösedagh near Sivas.
1244	Jerusalem taken by Khwarazmian troops.
1249	Seventh Crusade, led by Louis IX, landed at Damietta.
1250-1517	Mamlūk dynasty in Egypt.
1250	Shajar al-Durr, female ruler of Egypt.
1256	Hūlāgū took Assassin stronghold of Alamūt.
1256-1249	Īl-Khānid dynasty of Persia.
1258	Feb.: Hūlāgū sacked Baghdad and ended ᶜAbbāsid caliphate.
1260	Sept. 3: Mamlūk victory at ᶜAyn Jālūt over Mongols.
1260-1277	Reign of Baybars, Mamlūk sultan.
1265	Death of Hūlāgū.
1271	Journey of Marco Polo through Persia to China.
1273	Death of mystic, Jalāl al-Dīn al-Rūmī.
1274	Death of astronomer, Nāṣir al-Dīn al-Tūsī.
1279-1290	Reign of Qalā'ūn, Mamlūk sultan.
1282	Death of biographer, Ibn Khallikān.
1291	Fall of last Crusader stronghold in Levant, during Mamlūk sultanate of al-Ashraf Khalīl [1290-1293].
1291	Death of poet, Saᶜdī.
1294	Marco Polo in Persia on return to Europe.
1295-1304	Reign of Ghāzān Khān, Īl-Khānid ruler.
1317-1335	Reign of Abū Saᶜīd, Īl-Khānid ruler.
1318	Death of historian, Rashīd al-Dīn.
1324-1360	Reign of Orhān, Ottoman sultan.
1326	Ottomans captured Bursa.
1328	Death of Hanbalite, Ibn Taymīyyah.
1331	Ottoman conquest of Nicaea [Iznik].
1337	Ottoman conquest of Nicomedia [Izmit].
1345	First Ottoman campaign in Europe.
1354	Ottoman conquest of Ankara.
	Ottoman occupation of Gallipoli.
c.1360-89	Reign of Murād I, Ottoman sultan.
1361	Murād captured Adrianople [Edirne].
1369	Tīmūr conquered Khurāsān and Transoxiana.
1371	Battle of Chermanon and Ottoman victory over Serbs.
1378-1469	Qara Qoyunlu [Black Sheep] dynasty in Armenia and Azerbaijan.
1378-1502	Aq Qoyunlu [White Sheep] dynasty in Iraq and Armenia.
1382-1517	Circassian or Burjī Mamlūk rule of Egypt and Syria.
1382-1398	Reign of Barqūq, Mamlūk sultan.
1385	Ottoman conquest of Sofia.
1386	Ottoman conquest of Nish.
1387	Ottoman conquest of Salonika.
1389	June 15: Battle of Kosovo and Ottoman victory over Serbs.
	Death of poet, Ḥāfiẓ.

1389-1402	Reign of Bāyezīd I, Ottoman sultan.
1391-1398	First Ottoman siege of Constantinople.
1395	June: Wallachia became an Ottoman vassal state.
1396	Sept. 25: Battle of Nicopolis. Ottoman victory over Venice, Hungary, and other West Europeans.
1397	Ottomans annexed Karamān lands, including Konya.
1398	Ottoman conquest of Vidin in Europe and Sivas in Anatolia.
1398-1399	Tīmūr attacked India and sacked Delhi.
1400-1401	Tīmūr attacked Syria and Asia Minor. Captured Sivas.
1402	July 28: Battle of Ankara. Tīmūr captured Bāyezīd.
1402-1413	Civil war primarily among Bāyezīd's sons: Süleymān, Meḥmed and ᶜĪsā.
1403	Ottomans lost Salonika. Death of Bāyezīd.
1405	Feb. 18: Death of Tīmūr.
1405-1447	Reign of Shāh Rukh of the Tīmūrids.
1406	Death of Ibn Khaldūn, historian.
1413	Meḥmed I unified Ottoman territories.
1415	Meḥmed reconquered Smyrna [Izmir].
1418-1422	Revolt of Muṣṭafā the False [Düzme Muṣṭafā].
1421-1451	Reign of Murād II, Ottoman sultan.
1422	Second Ottoman siege of Constantinople.
1422-1437	Reign of Barsbāy, Mamlūk sultan.
1425-1430	Ottoman-Venetian War.
1430	Ottomans reconquered Salonika.
1440	Ottomans failed to take Belgrade.
1442	Death of historian, al-Maqrīzī.
1443	Iskender Beğ [Scanderbeğ/Georges Kastriote] rebelled in northern Albania.
1444	Murād II abdicated in favor of Meḥmed II. Nov. 10: Battle of Varna; Ottoman defeat of Hungarian King Ladislas and John Hunyadi.
1446	Murād II's second accession to Ottoman sultanate.
1448	Oct. 17-19: Second Battle of Kosovo. Ottomans defeated Hungarians.
1449	Death of ruler and astronomer, Ulugh Beğ.
1451	Feb. 3: Death of Murād II.
1451-1481	Reign of Meḥmed II, Ottoman sultan.
1452	Ottoman fortress of Rumeli Hisari erected.
1453	Apr. 6-May 29: Ottoman siege and capture of Constantinople.
1455	Ottomans made Moldavia a tribute state.
1456	Ottomans failed again to take Belgrade.
1459	Ottomans' final defeat of Serbs after death of George Brankovich.
1460	Meḥmed II conquered Morea.
1461	Ottoman conquest of Trebizond.
1463-1479	Ottoman-Venetian War.
1464	Completion of Topkapı Sarayı in Istanbul.
1466-1470	Inconclusive war between Mamlūks and Ottomans.
1468	Meḥmed II re-annexed Karamān lands in Anatolia. Jan. 17: Death of Iskender Beğ.
1468-1496	Reign of Qāyitbāy, Mamlūk sultan.
1469	Death of historian, Ibn Taghrī Birdī.
1471-1478	Uzun Ḥasan, Aq Qoyunlu ruler, sought European support against Ottomans.
1472	Venetian, Cypriot and Uzun Ḥasan alliance against Ottomans.
1475	Ottoman conquest of Genoese colonies in Crimea. Ottoman suzerainty over khānate of Crimea.
1479	Ottoman-Venetian peace.
1480-1481	Ottomans occupied Otranto, Italy.
1481	May 3: Death of Meḥmet II. May 20: Accession of Bāyezīd II. June 20: Battle of Yenisehir. Bāyezīd II defeated Cem, his brother and rival.
1481-1512	Reign of Bāyezīd II, Ottoman sultan.
1483	Ottomans annexed Herzegovina.
1484	Ottomans annexed Kilia and Akkerman.

1487	Bartholomew Diaz rounded Cape of Good Hope by vessel.
1492	Fall of Naṣrid dynasty in Granada to Christians.
	Death of ṣūfī poet, Jāmī.
1495	Feb. 25: Death of Ottoman, Prince Cem, in Naples.
1497	Bābur, eventual founder of Mughal dynasty, captured Samarqand.
1499	Ismāᶜīl came out of hiding and 1501 established Safavid dynasty.
	Ottoman conquest of Lepanto.
1499-1502	Ottoman war with Venice.
1500-1516	Reign of Qānṣūh al-Ghawrī, Mamlūk sultan.
1502	Safavid capital established at Tabriz.
1504	Safavid Shāh Ismāᶜīl took Baghdad.
1505	Bābur established Mughal dynasty in India.
	Death of encyclopedist, al-Suyūtī.
1506	Death of painter, Bihzād.
1507	Portuguese attacked Hormuz.
1509-1512	Increasing struggle for power primarily among Bāyezīd's sons: Korkūd, Aḥmed and Selīm.
1511	Rebellion of Shāh Kuli in Anatolia.
1512-1520	Reign of Selīm I, Ottoman sultan after deposing his father, Bāyezīd II.
1512	Withdrawal of Bābur from Central Asia.
1514	Aug. 23: Selīm I defeated Shāh Ismāᶜīl and his Qizilbash troops at Chāldirān.
1516	Portuguese, under d'Albuquerque, took Hormuz.
	Aug. 24: Ottoman victory over Mamlūks at Marj Dābiq.
1517	Jan.: Ottoman conquest of Egypt.
1520-1566	Reign of Süleymān I, Ottoman sultan.
1521	Ottoman conquest of Belgrade.
1522	Ottoman conquest of Rhodes.
1524-1525	Revolt of Aḥmad Pāshā in Egypt; suppressed by Ibrāhīm, Ottoman Grand Vezir.
1524-1576	Reign of Ṭahmāsp, Safavid shah.

1526	Aug. 29: Ottoman victory over Hungarians at Battle of Mohács.
1528	Ottomans captured Buda.
1529	Sept.-Oct.: Ottoman siege of Vienna.
1530	Death of Bābur.
1533	Armistice of Istanbul between Süleymān and Hapsburg Archduke Ferdinand.
	War between Safavids and Ottomans.
	Barbarossa made Ottoman Grand Admiral.
1534	Ottomans captured Tabriz and Baghdad.
1535	Ottoman-French alliance.
1537-1540	Ottoman-Venetian War.
1541	Ottomans annexed Central Hungary.
1547	Ottoman-Hapsburg peace.
1548	Ottoman-Safavid War.
1550	Süleymāniye mosque built by Sinan in Istanbul.
1551-1562	Ottoman-Hapsburg War.
1552	Ottomans failed to dislodge Portuguese from Hormuz.
1553-1555	Ottoman war with Safavids.
1555	May 29: Ottoman-Safavid Peace Treaty at Amasya.
	Revolt against Süleymān in name of executed son, known as the second Düzme [False] Muṣṭafā.
1558-1560	Struggle for power between Süleymān's sons, Selīm and Bāyezīd.
1561	Ṭahmāsp made Qazvīn Safavid capital.
1566	Sept. 6: Süleyman's death before fortress of Szigetvar.
1566-1574	Reign of Selīm II, Ottoman sultan.
1569	Ottoman campaign against Russians.
	Ottoman campaign in Yemen.
1571	Ottoman conquest of Famagusta, Cyprus.
	Oct. 7: Ottoman naval loss to Holy League at Lepanto.
1578	Ottomans annexed Georgia and Derbent.
1578-1639	Ottoman-Safavid wars.
1588-1629	Reign of ᶜAbbās I, Safavid shah.
1590	Ottoman-Safavid peace.
1593-1606	Ottoman-Hapsburg War.
1596-1610	Major problem with *celali* in Anatolia.

1600	Shāh ᶜAbbās made Iṣfahān the Ṣafavid capital.
	Death of Ottoman poet, Bāzī.
1602	Shāh ᶜAbbās captured Baḥrain from the Portuguese.
1603	Shāh ᶜAbbās captured Tabriz.
1606	Ottoman-Austrian Peace Treaty at Zsitvatorok.
1622	English captured Hormuz.
1623	Shāh ᶜAbbās I captured Baghdad.
1638	Ottomans recaptured Baghdad.
1639	Ottoman-Ṣafavid Peace Treaty of Zuhāb [Qaṣr-i Shīrīn].
1645	Ottomans attacked Crete.
1645-1670	Ottoman-Venetian War.
1656	Venice conquered Lemnos.
1656-1661	Meḥmed Köprülü, Ottoman Vezir.
1661-1676	Aḥmed Köprülü, Ottoman Vezir.
1663	Austria joined Venice against Ottomans.
1664	Ottomans defeated at St. Gotthard.
	20-year truce concluded at Vasvár with Austria.
1669	Conclusion of Ottoman-Venetian conflict by capitulation of Qandiya.
1672-1676	Ottoman-Polish War.
1676	Peace of Zurawno.
	Ottomans gained Podolia and Eastern Ukraine from Poland.
1676-1683	Kara Muṣṭafā, Ottoman Grand Vezir.
1677-1681	First Ottoman-Russian War.
1679	Death of Ottoman traveler, Evliya Chelebi.
1681	Peace of Radzyn.
	Ottomans lost Eastern Ukraine.
1683	July-Sept.: 2nd siege of Vienna. Ottoman defeat.
1684	Holy League of Papacy, Austria, Poland and Venice against Ottomans.
1686	Ottomans lost Buda to Austria.
	Venice captured most of Morea.
	Russia joined the Holy League.
1687	Ottomans lost Battle of Mohács to Austrians.
	First Russian siege of Azov.

1688	Ottomans lost Belgrade.
1689	Ottomans lost Szigetvár and Vidin.
	Muṣṭafā Köprülü, Ottoman Grand Vezir.
1690	Ottomans gained land against Austria, including Belgrade.
1691	Battle of Szalánkamén.
	Ottomans lost to Austria.
	Death of Fāẓil Muṣṭafā Köprülü.
1696	Russians, under Peter the Great, took Azov.
1697	Ottomans defeated at Zenta by Prince Eugene of Savoy.
1699	Jan. 26: Peace of Carlowitz.
	First permanent loss of territory by Ottomans to Europeans.
1703	July-Aug.: Edirne [Adrianople] Affair [vaqᶜasi] against Sulṭān Muṣṭafā II, forcing his abdication.
1710-1711	Ottoman-Russian War.
1711	Ottomans won Battle of Pruth against Russians; regained Azov.
	Peace of Pruth.
1716	Ottoman-Austrian War.
1716-1718	War with Venice; Ottomans retook Morea.
1717	Austrian conquest of Belgrade.
1718	Peace of Passarowitz.
	Ottomans lost lands to Austria.
1718-1730	Tulip Period [Lâle Devri] in Ottoman Empire.
1722	Mar. 8: Battle of Gulnābād. Ṣafavid forces routed by Afghan Maḥmūd.
	Peter the Great took Derbent.
	Afghan Maḥmūd took Iṣfahān.
	Effective end of Ṣafavid dynasty.
1725-1730	Ismāᶜīl Pāshā al-ᶜAẓm, Governor of Damascus.
1726-1729	Ottomans attacked Persia, but peace was arranged by Ashrāf, Afghan shah of Persia.
1729-1730	Nādir Khān Afshār drove Afghans from Persia.
1729	First Turkish printing press.
1736-1739	Ottoman war with Austria and Russia.

1736	Russia retook Azov.
1736-1747	Nādir Khān became Nādir Shāh.
1739	Treaty of Belgrade with Austria.
	Ottomans acquired Belgrade.
	Nādir Shāh attacked Delhi in India.
1740	Nādir Shāh attacked Bukhara.
1745	Establishment of Wahhābī Reform Movement in Dar^cīya, Arabia.
1747	Assassination of Nādir Shāh.
1750-1779	Karīm Khān Zand, sole ruler in southern Iran.
1757-1773	Reign of Muṣṭafā III, Ottoman sultan.
1758-1779	Karīm Khān Zand, undisputed ruler of Persia.
1768-1774	Ottoman-Russian War.
1769	Russians captured Jassy and Bucharest.
1770	Russian naval victory over Ottomans at Chesme.
1763-1773	^cAlī Bey active in Egypt.
1770-1789	Yūsuf Shihāb, Amīr of Lebanon.
1773-1789	Reign of ^cAbdülhamīd I, Ottoman sultan.
1774	Treaty of Küçük Kaynarci between Russia and Ottomans.
1775	Aḥmad Pāshā al-Jazzār [d. 1804], Governor of Sidon; later of Acre.
1783	Russia annexed Crimea.
1787-1792	Ottoman-Russian War.
1788	Austria joined Ottoman-Russian War.
1789	Austria invaded Bosnia and Serbia.
	Russia invaded Moldavia and Wallachia.
1789-1807	Reign of Selīm III, Ottoman sultan.
1789-1840	Bashīr II Shihāb, Amīr of Lebanon.
1791	Peace of Sistova between Austria and Ottomans re-establishing 1788 borders.
1792	Peace of Jassy between Russia and Ottomans, with Dniester as new Russian-Ottoman border.
1796	Āghā Muḥammad Qājār became Shāh of Persia.
1797-1834	Reign of Fatḥ ^cAlī, Qājār ruler.
1798	July: Bonaparte's victory at Battle of Pyramids outside Cairo.
	July: Admiral Nelson destroyed French fleet at Abū Qir.
1799	Napoleon invaded Palestine, but failed to capture Acre.
1800	Russia annexed Georgia.
1801	French evacuation of Egypt.
1802	Wahhābī raid on Karbala.
1803-1804	Wahhābīs captured Mecca and Medina.
1804	Serbian revolt.
1805-1848	Muḥammad ^cAlī, Viceroy of Egypt.
1806-1812	Ottoman-Russian War.
1807	Treaty of Finkenstein between Persia and Russia.
	Treaty of Tilsit between Napoleon and Russia.
	British occupation of Alexandria.
1808-1839	Reign of Maḥmūd II, Ottoman sultan.
1811	Mar. 1: Massacre of Egyptian Mamlūks by Muḥammad ^cAlī.
1811-1818	Muḥammad ^cAlī's campaigns against the Wahhābīs.
1813	Treaty of Gulistan between Persia and Russia.
1815-1817	Second Serbian uprising.
1816-1831	Dā'ūd Pāshā, Governor of Baghdad.
1818	Persian attack on Afghanistan.
1820s	British pacts with Persian Gulf *shaykhs*.
1820-1821	Sudanese campaigns of Muḥammad ^cAlī.
1821	Insurrections in Wallachia.
1821-1823	Ottoman-Persian War.
1821-1830	Greek War of Independence.
ca.1822	Establishment of Būlāq press in Egypt.
1823	Khartoum founded.
1824-1827	Muḥammad ^cAlī's campaigns in Greece led by Ibrāhīm.
1825-1828	Persian-Russian War.
1826	June 15: Massacre of Janissaries in Istanbul.
1827	Establishment of medical schools in Istanbul and Cairo.
	July 6: Treaty of London [Britain, France, Russia] on their support of Greece against Ottomans.
	Oct. 20: Battle of Navarino. Ottoman-Egyptian navy defeated by

Admiral Codrington and Western forces.

1828   Egyptians evacuated Greece.
        Treaty of Turkmanchai between Persia and Russia.

1828-1829 Ottoman-Russian War.

1829   Sept.: Treaty of Edirne between Ottomans and Russians.

1830   French invaded Algeria.

1832   Battle of Konya.
        Ottomans defeated by Egyptians.

1832-1841 Egyptian involvement in Syria under Ibrāhīm.

1833   Apr. 8: Convention of Kütahya between Ottomans and Egyptians.
        July 8: Treaty of Hûnkär Iskelesi between Ottomans and Russians.

1834   Arabic press in Beirut established.

1837-1838 Persian siege of Herat.

1839   June 24: Battle of Nezib.
        Ibrāhīm's victory over Ottoman forces trained by von Moltke.

1839   Nov. 3: Promulgation of Hatt-i Sherif Gülhane in Istanbul.

1839-1861 Reign of ᶜAbdülmecīd, Ottoman sultan.

1840   July: Treaty of London [Britain, Austria, Prussia, Russia] on Eastern question.

1841   Feb.: Hereditary viceroyalty of Egypt for Muḥammad ᶜAlī.
        July: Straits Convention [Britain, France, Prussia, Russia, Austria].

1842   Shihābī amirate of Lebanon ended.

1842-1858 Stratford de Redcliffe, British ambassador in Istanbul.

1843   Dual Qaimaqamate in Lebanon established.

1844   Sayyid Muḥammad ᶜAlī of Persia proclaimed himself the Bāb. This is considered the beginning of the Bahā'i Movement.

1848-1854 ᶜAbbās Ḥilmī I, Viceroy of Egypt.

1848-1896 Nāṣir al-Dīn, Qājār shah.

1850   Execution of the Bāb.
        Bābī uprisings.

1852   Persecution in Iran of Bābīs, who fled to the West.

1853   Oct.: Ottomans declared war on Russia.

1854-1856 Crimean War [Ottoman-Russian War], with a number of European states participating on the Ottoman side.

1854   Oct. 25: Battle of Balaklava and "Charge of the Light Brigade."
        Nov.: Ferdinand de Lesseps received concessions to build Suez Canal.

1854-1863 Saᶜīd, Viceroy of Egypt.

1855   Sept.: Sebastopol taken from Russia.

1856   Feb. 18: Hatt-i Hümayun promulgated in Istanbul.
        Feb.-Mar.: Treaty of Paris ending Crimean War.
        Persian occupation of Herat.

1857   Alexandria-Cairo railroad completed.
        Afghanistan's independence recognized by Britain and Persia.

1860   Robert College founded in Istanbul.

1860-1861 Civil war in Lebanon.
        French expeditionary force in Lebanon.

1861   Organic Regulation of Lebanon that established semi-autonomous self-government in Mt. Lebanon area.

1861-1876 Reign of ᶜAbdülazīz, Ottoman sultan.

1863-1879 Ismāᶜīl, Viceroy and then Khedive of Egypt.

1864   Ottoman Law of Vilayets.

1865   Establishment of Ottoman National Debt Administration.

1866   Ismāᶜīl of Egypt acquired "Khedive" title from Ottoman sultan.
        American University of Beirut, originally called Syrian Protestant College, founded.

1866-1868 Uprising on Crete against Ottomans.

1869   University of Istanbul founded.
        Nov. 17: Suez Canal officially opened.

1869-1872 Midhad Pāshā, Governor of Baghdad.

1872   Sweeping Persian concessions to Baron Julius de Reuter revoked by Qājār government.

1874-1879 Gen. Charles Gordon, Governor of Sudan.

1875   Establishment of Mixed Courts in Egypt.
        Britain acquired Khedive's shares in the Suez Canal Company.

1875   Uprisings in Herzegovina and Bosnia.

1876   May: Establishment of *Caisse de la
            Dette* and dual control in Egypt.
            ᶜAbdülazīz, Ottoman sultan, deposed.
            Aug.: Murād V, Ottoman sultan, deposed.
            Dec. 23: ᶜAbdülḥamīd, Ottoman sultan,
            promulgated a Constitution.

1876-1909   Reign of ᶜAbdülḥamīd, Ottoman sultan.

1877   Feb.: Midhad Pāshā dismissed from
            Ottoman government.
            Mar.: Opening of Ottoman Parliament.

1877-1878   Ottoman-Russian War.

1878   Feb. 13: Ottoman Parliament dismissed;
            Constitution suspended.
            Mar.: Treaty of San Stefano between
            Ottomans and Russians.
            June-July: Congress of Berlin modi-
            fied Treaty of San Stefano.
            Uprising in Crete.
            Russians organized Cossack Brigade in
            Persia.

1879-1892   Muḥammad Tawfīq, Khedive of Egypt.

1881   French occupied Tunisia.
            Outbreak of Sudanese Mahdia.

1882   First Zionist *Aliya* to Palestine.

1881-1882   ᶜUrābi revolt in Egypt.

1882   Jan. 8: British-French Gambetta Note
            on developments in Egypt.
            July: British bombarded and occupied
            Alexandria.
            Sept.: British defeated Egyptians at
            Battle of Tall al-Kābir.

1883   Nov.: General Hicks and Egyptian
            forces defeated by Mahdī.

1883-1907   Lord Cromer, British Consul General in
            Egypt.

1885   Mahdists captured Khartoum.
            Death of General Gordon.

1888   Convention of Constantinople concern-
            ing Suez Canal.

1889   Uprising in Crete.
            Imperial Bank of Persia founded.

1890-   Persian tobacco concession.

1890-1897   Armenian revolts against Ottomans.

1890-1898   Reconquest of the Sudan by Kitchener.

1892-1914   Reign of ᶜAbbās Ḥilmī II, Khedive of
            Egypt.

1896-1897   Uprising in Crete.

1896-1907   Muẓaffar al-Dīn, Qājār ruler.

1897   Ottoman-Greek War.

1898   Fashoda Incident.

1899   Anglo-Egyptian Condominium established
            in the Sudan.
            Concessions by Ottomans to Germans to
            build railroads.
            British agreement with *shaykh* of
            Kuwait.

_____

1900   First Persian oil concession to d'Arcy.

1900-1908   Hejaz railroad built.

1901   Ibn Saᶜud and Wahhābīs took Riyadh.

1902   Congress of Ottoman Liberals met in
            Paris.

1902-1903   Uprising in Macedonia.

1904   Apr.: Entente Cordiale between Brit-
            ain and France.

1905   Persian Revolution.
            Death of Muḥammad ᶜAbdūh.

1906   May: Sinai officially part of Egypt
            after Taba-Aqaba frontier dispute
            between Ottomans and Britain.
            Jun. 13: Dinshawāy Incident in Egypt.
            Aug.: Qājār ruler, Muẓaffar al-Dīn,
            promulgated a Constitution.
            Dec.: Persian Constitution ratified.

1907   Anglo-Russian Convention divided
            Persia.
            Young Turk movements united under name
            of Committee of Union and Progress.

1907-1909   Muḥammad ᶜAlī, Qājār ruler.

1907-1911   Gorst, British Consul General in Egypt.

1908   Revolt of Ottoman Third Army Corps in
            Salonika.
            ᶜAbdülḥamīd reactivated 1876 Consti-
            tution.
            Crete annexed by Greece.
            Death of Egyptian political leader,
            Muṣṭafā Kāmil.

1909   Apr.: Ottoman Third Army deposed
            ᶜAbdülḥamīd II.

1909	Formation of Anglo-Persian Oil Company to exploit d'Arcy concession.
	Russian intervention in Persia.
1909-1924	Aḥmad, Qājār ruler.
1910	Assassination of Buṭrus Ghālī in Egypt.
	Uprising in Albania against Ottomans.
1911	Shuster, American financial expert, appointed as Persian Treasurer General; dismissed after Russian intervention.
	Abadan refinery completed.
1911-1912	Ottoman-Italian War over Libya and Ottoman loss.
1911-1914	Kitchener, British Consul General in Egypt.
1912	Proclamation of Albanian independence.
1912-1913	First Balkan War.
1913	Committee of Union and Progress [CUP] took over direct control of Ottoman government.
	Arab Congress in Paris.
	Second Balkan War.
	Sept.: Treaty of Constantinople between Ottomans and Bulgaria.
1914	Formation of Arab *al-ᶜAhd*, Nationalist secret society.
	Aug.: Secret treaty between CUP and Germany.
	Aug.: Outbreak of World War I.
	Nov. 1: Ottomans declared war on Britain, France and Russia.
	Nov. 5: Britain declared war on Ottomans and annexed Cyprus.
	Nov. 22: British forces landed at Fao, Iraq.
	Dec. 18: British declared a protectorate over Egypt.
1914-1917	Husayn Kāmil, Sultan of Egypt.
1915	Feb.: Ottomans attacked Suez Canal.
	Mar. 18: Constantinople Agreement among Britain, France and Russia on division of Ottoman lands.
	Apr. 25: Allied landing on Gallipoli Peninsula.
	Apr. 26: Treaty of London among Britain, France, Russia and Italy.
	July: Husayn-MacMahon correspondence began.
	Sep. 28: Turks laid siege to British at Kūt al-Amāra, Iraq.
	Oct. 24: Major British reply to Husayn's proposals.
	Dec.: Agreement between Britain and Ibn Saᶜūd.
1916	Jan. 9: Allied withdrawal from Gallipoli Peninsula.
	Apr. 29: British surrendered to Turks at Kūt al-Amāra, Iraq.
	May: Sykes-Picot Agreement.
	Jun. 5: Arab Revolt, popularly associated in the West with T.E. Lawrence [Lawrence of Arabia].
	Jul. 19: 2nd Ottoman campaign against Suez Canal.
	Dec. 15: British recognized Husayn as King of the Hejaz only.
1917	Mar. 11: British occupied Baghdad.
	Mar.-Apr.: British battled Ottomans in Gaza.
	Apr.: Agreement of St. Jean de Maurene among Britain, Italy, France.
	Nov. 2: Balfour Declaration.
	Nov. 7: Bolshevik Revolution in Russia.
	Dec. 5: Soviets renounced all claims to Ottoman lands.
	Dec. 9: Allenby took Jerusalem.
1917-1936	Aḥmad Fuᶜād, King of Egypt.
1918	Mar. 3: Treaty of Brest Litovsk between Soviets and Central Powers.
	Oct. 1: British and Arabs captured Damascus.
	Oct. 7: French troops landed at Beirut.
	Oct. 26: Aleppo captured by British and Arabs.
	Oct. 30: Mudros Armistice concluded between Ottomans and Allies.
	Nov. 11: Armistice in Europe.
	Nov.: Zaghlūl, Egyptian leader, led

wafd to British High Commissioner.

Nov. 13: Allied fleet arrived in
Istanbul.

1919   Jan.: Peace conference opened in
Paris.

Feb.: Greek Premier Venizelos issued
claims to Izmir and part of Anatolia.

Mar. 8: Zaghlūl deported from Egypt.
Popular uprising.

Mar.: Italians landed in Anatolia.

May: Ibn Sa\u1d defeated troops of
Husayn of Mecca.

May 15: Greeks landed at Izmir
[Smyrna].

May 19: Muṣṭafā Kemal [b. 1880]
arrived at Samsun.

Jul.23: Turkish Nationalist Congress
at Erzurum.

Aug. 9: Anglo-Persian Agreement;
never ratified by Persian *majlis*.

Sep.13: Turkish National Pact at
Sivas; declaration of National Pact.

Oct.: General Gouraud, French High
Commissioner for Lebanon and Syria.

Dec.: Lord Milner's mission to Egypt.

1920   Mar. 20: Syrian National Congress
proclaimed Fayṣal King of Syria
and Palestine.

Apr.: Provisional Turkish government
established in Ankara.
San Remo Conference,

May: Soviets in Gilan.

July: Sir Herbert Samuel, High Commissioner for Palestine.
French occupation of Damascus.

Jul.-Aug.: Major Arab insurrection in
Iraq.

Aug.: Ibn Sa\u1d annexed \uAsīr.

Aug. 20: Ottoman government in Istanbul signed Treaty of Sèvres.

Aug. 31: French High Commissioner
created Greater [Modern] Lebanon.

1921   Jan. 20: Turkish Fundamental Law
adopted by Grand National Assembly
in Ankara.

Feb. 21: Persian *coup d'état*, led by
Reza Khān.

Feb. 26: Russo-Persian Treaty signed.

Mar.: Cairo Conference run by Winston
Churchill.

Mar. 13: Italians agreed to withdraw
from Turkey.

Mar. 16: Treaty of Moscow between
Soviets and Muṣṭafā Kemal.

Apr. 1: \uAbdullāh, ruler of newly
created State of Transjordan.

May: Major anti-Zionist riots in
Palestine.

Aug. 23: Fayṣal proclaimed King of
Iraq.

Aug.24-Sep.16: Battle of Sakarya between Turks and Greeks.

Oct. 20: French agreed to withdraw
from Turkey.

1922   Feb. 28: Britain declared Egyptian
independence.

Mar. 15: Fu\uād took title of King of
Egypt.

July: Churchill's White Paper for
Palestine.

Jul. 24: League of Nations approved
British and French mandates for
Palestine, Transjordan, Iraq,
Lebanon and Syria.

Sep. 11: Turks retook Izmir.

Nov. 1: Muṣṭafā Kemal abolished
the sultanate.

Nov. 20: Lausanne Conference began,
with Turkish delegation headed by
İsmet.

1922-1927 First Millspaugh mission to Iran.

1923   Apr.: Egyptian Constitution promulgated.

Jul. 24: Treaty of Lausanne signed
with Turkey.

Sep. 29: Mandate system came into
official effect.

Oct. 13: Ankara made Turkey's capital.

Oct. 29: Turkish republic formally
proclaimed.

1924   Mar. 3: Caliphate abolished.
          Oct. 3: Ḥusayn of Mecca abdicated in
                   favor of his son, ᶜAlī.
          Nov. 22: Sir Lee Stack murdered in
                   Egypt.
                   Allenby's ultimatum.
1924-1927 Druze rebellions in Syria.
1925   Apr.: Hebrew University in Jerusalem
                 opened.
          Aug.: Polygamy abolished in Turkey.
          Oct.: Persian *majlis* deposed last
                 Qājār shāh.
          Nov.: Wearing of *fez* in Turkey for-
                 bidden.
          Dec. 12: Reza Khān became Reza Shāh,
                   founder of Pahlavi dynasty of Iran.
          Dec. 19: ᶜAlī, King of the Hejaz,
                    abdicated.
1926   Jan.: Ibn Saᶜud proclaimed King of
                 the Hejaz.
          Apr.: Reza Shāh crowned himself.
1927   Death of Zaghlūl.
          Egyptian *wafd*, headed by al-Naḥḥās.
          European dress required for men in
          Iran.
          May: British recognized Ibn Saᶜud's
                kingdom.
1928   Apr.: Turkey declared a secular state.
          Nov.: Turkey adopted Latin alphabet.
          Abolition of capitulations in Iran.
1929   Aug.: Wailing Wall Incident.
                 Riots in Palestine.
1930   Mar.: Official "Turkification" of all
                 Turkish city names.
          May: Shaw Report for Palestine.
          Oct.: Passfield's White Paper for
                 Palestine.
1931   Feb.: British Prime Minister
                 MacDonald's letter on Palestine.
1932   Aug.: Turkey joined League of Nations.
          Sep.: Saudi Arabia's new, official
                 name of Kingdom of the Hejaz and
                 Nejd.
          Oct.: Iraq joined League of Nations.
1933   Sep.: Death of Fayṣal of Iraq.

1933-1939 Reign of Ghāzī, who succeeded Fayṣal
          in Iraq.
1934   Jan. 1: Muṣṭafā Kemal became Atatürk.
          Jan. 1: Family names required of all
                   Turkish citizens.
1935   Mar. 21: Iran became official name
                    for Persia.
          Oct. 3:   Italians invaded Ethiopia.
1936   Apr.-Oct.: General strike of Arabs in
                     Palestine.
          July: Montreaux Convention gave Tur-
                 key complete control of Straits of
                 Dardanelles.
          Aug. 26: Anglo-Egyptian Treaty.
          Sept. 9: Franco-Syrian Treaty; never
                    ratified.
          Oct. 29: First military *coup d'état*
                    in Iraq, led by Bakr Ṣidqī.
1936-1952 Reign of King Fārūq of Egypt, includ-
          ing period of his minority.
1937   Jul. 8: Peel Commission Report on
                   Palestine.
          Jul. 9: Saadabad Pact among Iran,
                   Iraq, Afghanistan and Turkey.
          Sep. 8: Pan-Arab Congress at Bludan.
1938   Nov. 9: Woodhead Commission Report
                   on Palestine.
          Nov. 10: Atatürk died; succeeded by
                   Ismet Inönü as president of Turkey.
1939   Feb.: Anglo-Arab Conference on Pal-
                 estine, held in London.
          May 17: British White Paper on Pal-
                   estine.
          Jun. 23: Alexandretta [Hatay] Province
                   incorporated into Turkey.
          Sept.:   Outbreak of World War II with
                   German attack on Poland.
1940   Jun. 22: Franco-German armistice.
1941   Apr.-Jun.: Rashīd ᶜAlī in power in
                      Iraq; ended with British occupation.
          June: Allies occupied Syria and Leb-
                 anon; governed by Vichy adminis-
                 trators.
          Aug. 25: Anglo-Soviet troops moved
                    into Iran.

1941   Sep. 16: Reza Shāh of Iran forced to
          abdicate; succeeded by his son,
          Mohammed [Muḥammad] Reza Shāh.

1942   Feb. 4: Britain forced Egyptian gov-
          ernment to accept al-Naḥḥās as
          Prime Minister.
          May 11: Zionist Biltmore program.
          Jul. 1: Rommel's German army reached
          al-Alamayn, Egypt.
          Oct.: Germans defeated at al-Alamayn.

1943   Jan.: Germans defeated at Stalingrad.
          National Pact between Sunnī and Mar-
          onite leaders of Lebanon.
          Dec. 1: Tehran Declaration by Church-
          ill, Roosevelt and Stalin.

1943-1945 Millspaugh [American financial expert]
          mission to Iran.
          Oct. 5: "Protocol of Alexandria," is-
          used by Arab leaders, laid basis
          for Arab League.
          Nov. 4: Lord Moyne assassinated in
          Cairo by "Stern Gang."
          Dec.: Jebel Druze absorbed into
          Syrian state.

1945   Mar. 22: Arab League created.
          Nov.: Anglo-American Committee of
          Inquiry formed to investigate
          Palestine's future.
          Dec. 12: Proclamation of Autonomous
          Republic of Azerbaijan.

1946   Jan.: Democratic Party of Turkey
          founded.
          Jan. 19: Iran appealed to UN Security
          Council to have Soviet troops with-
          draw from Azerbaijan.
          Mar. 19: 2nd Iranian appeal to
          Security Council.
          May 1: Report issued by Anglo-American
          Committee of Inquiry on Palestine.
          May 9: Soviet troops evacuated from
          Iran.
          Dec.11: Collapse of Autonomous Repub-
          lic of Azerbaijan.

1947   Mar.12: Truman Doctrine to maintain
          governments in Greece and Turkey.

          May: UN Security Council on Palestine
          [UNSCOP] created.
          Oct. 22: Iranian *majlis* rejected Soviet-
          Iranian oil concession.
          Nov. 27: UN Partition Plan for Palestine
          passed by UN General Assembly.

1948   Apr. 10: Massacre of Arabs at Deir Yassin.
          May 14: State of Israel established.
          May 14-15: End of British Mandate for
          Palestine.
          May 15-Jun. 11: Open warfare between Arabs
          and Israelis.
          Jul. 8-18: 2nd phase of open warfare be-
          tween Arabs and Israelis.
          Sep. 17: Count Bernadotte assassinated by
          Stern Gang in Palestine.
          Nov. 19: Establishment of UNRPR.
          Dec. 1: ᶜAbdullāh renamed his state
          Ḥāshimite Kingdom of Jordan.

1949   Jan. 31: Jordan joined United Nations.
          Feb. 24: Israeli-Egyptian armistice.
          Mar. 7: Israeli-Lebanese armistice.
          Mar. 11: Israel joined United Nations.
          Mar. 30: Syrian *coup d'état*; civilian
          government of Shukrī al-Quwatlī replaced
          by Col. Ḥusnī Zaᶜīm.
          Apr. 3: Israel-Jordan armistice.
          Jul. 20: Israel-Syria armistice.
          Aug. 14: Syrian *coup d'état*, led by Col.
          Sāmī al-Ḥinnawī.
          Dec. 20: Syrian *coup d'état*, led by Col.
          Adīb Shīshaklī.

1950   Mar.: National Front, led by Dr. Mosaddeq,
          made significant gains in election for
          Iranian *majlis*.
          May 1: Democratic Party replaced People's
          Republic Party in Turkish election:
          Menderes as Prime Minister and Bayar as
          President.
          May 25: Britain, France and U.S. issued
          Tripartite Declaration.
          Sep. 19: Turkey joined North Atlantic
          Organization.

1951   Mar. 7: Iranian Prime Minister Razmara
          shot to death.

1951   Apr. 29: Dr. Muḥammad Mosaddeq became
               Iranian Prime Minister.

           May 2: Shāh of Iran signed oil national-
               ization bill.

           Jul. 20: King ᶜAbdullāh of Jordan assas-
               sinated.

           Dec. 24: Libya became independent.

1952   Jan. 25: British involved in Battle of
               Ismāᶜīlīya against Egyptian police.

           Jan. 26: "Black Saturday" in Cairo.

           Jul. 23: Egyptian Revolution, led by
               Gamāl ᶜAbd al-Nāṣir [Nasser] and RCC.

           Jul. 26: Fārūq compelled to abdicate.

           Aug. 3: Iranian *majlis* gave Prime Min-
               ister Muṣaddiq [Mosaddeq] unlimited
               powers for 6 months.

           Aug. 11: Ḥusayn [Hussein] became King
               of Jordan; replaced his father, Talāl.

           Sept.: Major Land Reform Act promulgated
               in Egypt.

1953   Jan. 19: Iranian *majlis* voted to extend
               Mosaddeq's [Muṣaddiq's] power for a
               year.

           Feb.: Angl-Egyptian agreement on British
               evacuation of Sudan.

           Jun. 18: RCC abolished Egyptian monarchy.

           Aug. 13: Iranian Shāh dismissed Mosaddeq.

           Aug. 16: Iranian Shāh fled to Iraq.

           Aug. 22: Iranian Shāh returned to power
               in Iran.

           Aug. 22: Mosaddeq placed under arrest.

           Nov. 3: Moshe Sharett became Prime Min-
               ister of Israel; replaced Ben-Gurion.

           Nov. 9: ᶜAbd al-ᶜAzīz b. Saᶜūd died.

           Nov. 9: Saᶜūd became King of Saudi
               Arabia.

1954   Feb. 24: Shīshaklī removed from power in
               Syria by military.

           Aug. 5: Compensation Agreement between
               Iran and AIOC.

           Oct. 19: Egyptian-British agreement on
               evacuation of British Suez bases.

           Oct. 26: Muslim Brotherhood attempted to
               assassinate Nasser.

           Nov. 1: Algerian rebellion began.

1955   Feb. 17: Ben-Gurion became Israel's
               Defense Minister.

           Feb. 24: Iraq-Turkey Agreement.
               Start of Baghdad Pact.

           Feb. 28: Israeli raid on Gaza.

           April: Britain joined Baghdad Pact.

           Apr. 18-24: Afro-Asian Conference at
               Bandung.

           Sept.: Pakistan joined Baghdad Pact.

           Sep. 27: Nasser announced Russian arms
               deal.

           Oct. 11: Iran officially joined Baghdad
               Pact.

           Nov. 3: Ben-Gurion became Prime Min-
               ister of Israel.

1956   Jan. 1: Proclamation of Sudanese inde-
               pendence.

           Mar. 1: Ḥusayn of Jordan removed Gen.
               John Glubb from command of Arab Legion.

           May 16: Egypt recognized government of
               Mainland China.

           Jul. 19: Secretary of State Dulles an-
               nounced no U.S. aid to build Egyptian
               Aswan High Dam.

           Jul. 26: Nasser nationalized Suez Canal Co.

           Oct. 11: Major Israeli raid against
               Jordan.

           Oct. 24: Jordan joined Egypt and Syria
               in a defense pact.

           Oct. 29: Israel invaded Sinai.

           Oct. 30: Anglo-French ultimatum issued
               to Egypt and Israel.

           Oct. 31: Britain bombed Egyptian mili-
               tary bases.

           Nov. 5: Israeli military operations in
               Sinai effectively ended.

           Nov. 5: Anglo-French force invaded
               Canal Zone.

           Nov. 6: Eden and Mollet accepted cease-
               fire, effective next day.

           Dec. 22: Withdrawal of Anglo-French con-
               tingents from Suez completed; replaced
               by UNEF troops.

1957   Jan. 5: Eisenhower Doctrine announced.

           Mar. 7: Last Israeli troops withdrew from

Sinai and Gaza Strip.

Mar. 13: Jordan terminated 1948 Anglo-Jordanian Treaty.

1958 Feb. 1: United Arab Republic [UAR] of Egypt and Syria created.

Apr.: Amīr Fayşal came to power in Saudi Arabia.

May: Increasing internal turmoil in Lebanon.

Jul. 14: Iraqi Revolution, led by al-Qāsim [Kassem].

Jul. 15: U.S. Marines landed in Lebanon.

Oct. 25: U.S. troops withdrew from Lebanon.

Nov. 17: Ibrāhīm ᶜAbbūd led coup in Sudan.

1960 May 27: Turkish military, led by General Gürsel, overthrew government of Celal Bayar and Adnan Menderes; established NUC.

1961 Jun. 19: Kuwait declared free and independent of British control.

Jun. 25: Iraqis threatened Kuwait.

July: Major socialization and nationalization laws promulgated in Egypt.

Sep. 28: Syria withdrew from UAR.

Oct. 25: 2nd Turkish republic established under President Gürsel.

1962 July: Algeria became independent.

July: Shāh of Iran announced White Revolution for internal reform.

1962 Sep. 19: Muḥammad al-Badr became Imām of Yemen.

Sep. 26: Beginning of Yemeni Civil War, with Republican forces led by ᶜAbdullāh Sallāl.

1963 Jan.: Aden joined Federation of South Arabia.

Feb. 8: Coup d'état in Iraq, led by ᶜAbd al-Salām ᶜArīf.

Mar. 8: Coup d'état in Syria, led by Baᶜthists.

Jun. 16: Levi Eshkol became Israeli Prime Minister.

1964 May 28: PLO established, with Aḥmad Shuqayri as head.

Nov. 2: Fayşal officially replaced Saᶜūd as Saudi Arabian king.

1965 Oct.: Süleymān Demirel, head of Justice Party, became Turkish Prime Minister.

1966 Feb. 23: Military coup in Syria, led by Gen. Şalāḥ Jadīd.

Mar. 28: Gen. Cevdet Sunay became President of Turkey.

Apr. 13: ᶜAbd al-Salām ᶜArīf of Iraq died in helicopter crash; succeeded by his brother, Maj. Gen. ᶜAbd al-Raḥmān ᶜArīf.

Oct.: Intra Bank of Beirut failed.

Nov. 13: Palestinian fidā'iyīn land mine killed Israelis near Hebron.

Nov. 13: Israeli reprisal attack on Jordanian border village of al-Samu.

1967 Apr. 7: Israeli-Syrian air clash.

May 14: Nasser reinforced Sinai forces.

May 16: Egyptian troops replaced UNEF in Sinai.

May 21: Partial mobilization of Israeli and Egyptian troops.

May 22: Nasser announced blockade of Straits of Tiran.

May 30: Jordan joined Arab Defense Pact of Egypt and Syria.

June 1: Moshe Dayan was made Israeli Defense Minister.

June 5: Arab-Israeli War began with Israeli air strikes.

Jun. 10: End of 3rd Arab-Israeli War [Six-Day War].

Jul. 28: Israel "annexed" Old Jerusalem.

Aug. 29-Sep. 1: Arab summit meeting at Khartoum.

Oct. 21: Egypt sank Israeli naval destroyer, Elath.

Oct. 22: Israel attacked Egyptian Suez oil refineries.

Nov. 4: ᶜAbd al-Raḥmān al-Iryānī led coup in Yemen against ᶜAbdullāh Sallāl.

Nov. 22: UN Resolution 242 on Arab-Israeli problem.

Nov. 30: Last British troops left Aden.

Dec. 24: Aḥmad Shuqary resigned as head of PLO.

1968 Mar. 21: Israel attacked Karameh, Jordan; fought against Palestinian and Jordanian troops.

Jul. 17: *Coup d'état* in Iraq.

Jul. 17: Gen. Aḥmad Ḥasan al-Bakr became President.

Jul. 23: El-Al Israel airliner hijacked to Algeria.

Oct. 26: Gen. Ḥāfiẓ al-Asad became Syrian leader in a bloodless *coup*.

Oct. 27: Israeli raided deep into Egyptian territory.

Dec. 26: PLO attacked El-Al Israel airliner in Athens.

Dec. 28: Israel raided Beirut airport; destroyed 13 planes.

1969 Feb. 3: Yāsir ᶜArafāt became head of the PLO.

Feb. 18: PLO attacked Israeli airliner in Zürich.

Feb. 28: Gen. Ḥāfiẓ al-Asad took over direct control of Syrian government.

Mar. 8: Intensive fighting along the Suez Canal.

Mar. 8: War of Attrition began; lasted until August 1970.

Mar. 17: Golda Meir became Israel's Prime Minister.

May: Gen. Jaᶜfar al-Numayrī seized power in Sudan.

June: PFLP blew up tapline in Golan Heights.

July 1: Israel moved major government offices to Old Jerusalem.

Aug. 11: Israel attacked Lebanese villages, which Israel claimed were *fidā'iyīn* bases.

Aug. 21: Fire at al-Aqsa Mosque in Jerusalem.

Aug. 29: TWA airliner hijacked by PLO *fidā'iyīn*.

Sep. 1: Revolution in Libya, led by Col. Muᶜammar al-Qadhdhāfī [Qaddafi].

Oct.: Palestinian-Lebanese clashes.

Nov.: Cairo Agreement between Lebanon and Palestine.

Dec. 9: U.S. Secretary of State Rodgers proposed Middle East peace plan.

1970 Feb. 12: Israeli jets raided Cairo suburbs.

Mar. 11: Major agreement between Iraqi government and the Kurds.

June: Widespread fighting in Jordan between Palestinian *fidā'iyīn* and Ḥusayn's troops.

Jul. 21: Aswan High Dam completed.

Jul. 26: Qabus b. Saᶜīd overthrew his father in palace *coup* in Oman.

Aug. 7: Cease-fire along Suez Canal between Egypt and Israel, ending the War of Attrition.

Sept.: Civil war in Jordan between Ḥusayn and Palestinian *fidā'iyīn*.

Sep. 6-12: PFLP hijacked and blew up U.S. and Swiss airlines in Jordan and Egypt.

Sep. 23: Süleymān Faranjiya became President of Lebanon.

Sep. 27: Truce in Jordan signed between Ḥusayn and Palestinian leader, ᶜArafāt.

Sep. 28: Gamāl ᶜAbd al-Nāṣir died.

Sep. 28: Anwar al-Sādāt became President of Egypt.

Sep. 29: Last hostages released from the September 6th hijacking.

Oct. 13: Second truce between Ḥusayn and ᶜArafāt signed.

Nov. 13: Gen. Ḥāfiẓ al-Asad consolidated his power in Syria.

1971 Mar. 7: Sadat ceased renewing Egyptian-Israeli Cease-Fire Agreement.

May 27: Soviet-Egyptian Treaty of Friendship signed.

Jul. 18: Last *fidā'iyīn* positions eliminated in Jordan.

Jul.19-22: *Coup d'état* in Sudan, led by Hāshim al-ᶜAtā, fell to counter-*coup*, led by Numayrī.

1972 Apr. 6: Soviet-Iraqi Treaty of Friendship signed.

May: Marxist-oriented, urban guerillas active in Turkey.

1972 May 30:   3 Japanese men, in name of Palestinian movement, opened fire on civil-
ians at Lod Airport, Tel Aviv; killed
26 persons.

Jul. 18: President Sadat of Egypt ordered
Soviet advisers and experts to leave
Egypt.

Sep. 5:   11 members of Israeli Olympic
team in Munich were killed while hostages of Palestinian *fidā'īyīn*.

Oct. 5:   OPEC set goal of 51% ownership
in oil companies.

1973 Feb. 21: Israel shot down Libyan civilian
airliner over Sinai.

Mar. 1:   Palestinian "Black Septemberists"
seized Saudi embassy in Khartoum; 3
American diplomats ultimately killed.

Mar. 26: Sadat announced Soviet-Egyptian
relations were again solid.

Apr. 6:   Fahri Korutürk elected President
of Turkey.

Apr. 10: Israeli commandos raided Sidon
and Beirut against PLO.

May: Malkert Agreement between PLO and
Lebanon on halting PLO raids from
Lebanon.

July 1:   Attempted overthrow of al-Bakr's
Iraqi government failed.

July 5:   President Ḥāfiẓ al-Asad of Syria
inaugurated Euphrates Dam at al-Tabqa,
which was renamed Madīnat al-Thawra.

Sep. 13: Air clashes between Israel and
Syria.

Oct. 6:   Egyptian and Syrian troops attacked Israeli forces; detachments from
other Arab states eventually joined in.

Oct. 14: U.S. began resupplying Israel to
balance continuing Soviet aid to Arabs.

Oct. 16: Israelis crossed Suez Canal.

Oct. 18: OAPEC announced cutback in oil
production; oil price was raised during
this period.

Oct. 22: UN Security Council passed Resolution 338, calling for a cease-fire
"in place."

Oct. 23: UN Security Council passed Resolution 339, reconfirming call for
cease-fire; Israel and Egypt accepted
it, while Syria accepted it "with con-
ditions."

Oct.25-31: United States troops on alert.

Oct. 27: UN observers on Suez front.

Oct. 28: Israeli-Egyptian negotiations
began at Kilometer 101 on Suez-Cairo
Road.

Nov. 5:   OAPEC announced embargo of all
oil to U.S. and Netherlands.

Nov.6-9: U.S. Secretary of State, Henry
Kissinger, traveled back and forth between Cairo and Jerusalem.

Nov. 11: Israel and Egypt signed a Cease-
Fire Accord; continued negotiations.

1974 Jan. 18: Israel and Egypt signed a Disengagement Agreement.

Mar. 5:   Israel completed withdrawal from
area west of Suez Canal.

Mar. 11: War of Attrition began between
Israel and Syria.

Mar. 18: Arab oil embargo of U.S. lifted.

May 29:   Israel and Syria agreed to a
Disengagement Agreement.

Jun. 13: Bloodless *coup* in Yemen, led by
Ibrāhīm al-Ḥamīdī.

Oct. 28: Arab League meeting at Rabat
recognized PLO as sole, legitimate
representative of Palestinian people.

Nov. 13: ᶜArafāt spoke before UN General
Assembly.

1975 Mar. 6:   International Border and Good
Neighborly Relations Treaty concluded
by Ṣaddām Ḥusayn and M. Reza Shāh.

Mar. 22: Collapse of Kissinger's "shuttle
diplomacy" mission.

Mar. 25: Saᶜūdī King Fayṣal assassinated.

Mar. 25: Khālid became king.

Apr. 13: Symbolic beginning of Lebanese
Civil War.

June 5:   Suez Canal reopened after 8
years.

Sep. 1:   Egyptian-Israeli Interim Agreement.

1975   Nov. 10: UN General Assembly resolution
          declared: "Zionism is a form of
          racism."

1976   Mar. 14: Sadat terminated 1971 Soviet-
          Egyptian Treaty.

        June: First official units of Syrian-
          dominated Arab Deterrent Force arrived
          in Lebanon.

        July 1: Abortive *coup* in Sudan against
          Numayrī.

        July 3: Israeli rescue raid on Entebbe
          Airport, Uganda.

        Aug. 12: Tall al-Za^ctar Palestinian ref-
          ugee camp fell to Phalangists after
          54-day siege.

        Sep. 23: Elias Sarkís became Lebanese
          President amidst civil war.

        Dec. 20: Yitzhak Rabin resigned as Prime
          Minister of Israel.

1977   May 18: Victory of Likud Party, with
          Menachem Begin as Israeli Prime Min-
          ister.

        July: Brief border war between Egypt and
          Libya.

        July: Shutra Agreement between PLO and
          Lebanon to restrict PLO activities and
          weapons in Lebanon.

        Nov. 9: Anwar al-Sādāt, Egypt's Presi-
          dent, flew to Israel.

        Dec.25-26: Begin and Sadat met in
          Ismā^cīlīya.

1978   Jan. 8: Major incident in Iran between
          demonstrators and police.

        Feb.17-21: Major riots in Tabriz against
          government.

        Mar. 11: Major Palestinian raid into
          Israel from southern Lebanon.

        Mar. 14: Large-scale military operation
          by Israel into Lebanon.

        Apr. 27: Hafizullāh Amīn and Nūr Muḥammad
          Tarakī overthrew government of Muḥammad
          Dā'ūd in Afghanistan.

        Apr. 27: Tarakī became President.

        June: Withdrawal of Israelis from south-
          ern Lebanon completed.

        Aug. 20: Movie house burned in Abadan;
          over 400 died.

        Sep. 8: "Black Friday" in Tehran, with
          deaths of large number of protestors.

        Sep. 17: Camp David accords for peace in
          Middle East; framework for conclusion
          of a peace treaty between Egypt and
          Israel.

        Oct. 6: Ayatollāh Rūḥallāh Khumaynī
          [Khomeini] expelled from Iraq.

        Nov.: Arab summit meeting rejected Egyp-
          tian-Israeli accord.

1979   Jan. 16: Shāh Moḥammed Reza Pahlavi left
          Iran.

        Jan. 31: Ayatollāh Khumaynī returned to
          Iran.

        Mar. 26: Peace treaty between Israel and
          Egypt signed in Washington, D.C.

        Mar. 31: Islamic republic established by
          referendum in Iran.

        Jul. 16: Ṣaddām Ḥusayn replaced Aḥmad
          Hasan al-Bakr as President of Iraq.

        Sep. 16: Hafizullāh Amīn overthrew gov-
          ernment of Nūr Muḥammad Tarakī in
          Afghanistan.

        Nov. 4: U.S. Embassy in Iran taken over,
          including a number of U.S. hostages.

        Nov. 6: Mehdi Bazargan, Iranian Prime
          Minister, resigned; Revolutionary
          Council took over Iran.

        Nov. 20: Revolt in Grand Mosque, Mecca.

        Dec. 27: Babrak Karmal made President of
          Afghanistan.

        Dec. 27: Hafizullāh Amīn assassinated.

        Dec. 27: Soviets invaded Afghanistan.

1980   Feb. 4: Banī-Ṣadr became first President
          of the Islamic Republic of Iran.

        Apr. 7-Sep. 12: Ihsan Sabri Çanǧlayangil,
          Acting President of Turkey.

        Apr. 24: U.S. military operation in Iran
          aborted.

        Jul. 9: Major Israeli air raid on Leb-
          anon.

        Jul. 27: Mohammed Reza Shāh died in Egypt.

        Jul. 30: Israeli Knesset declared all of

Jerusalem to be the united capital of Israel.

1980   Sep. 12:   Gen. Kenan Evren led military *coup* in Turkey.
                End of 2nd Turkish republic.

       Sep. 22:   Iraq invaded Iran.

       Oct.:   Soviet-Syrian Treaty of Friendship and Cooperation signed.

1981   Jan. 20:   Iran released American hostages after 444 days of captivity.

       Jan.25-28:   Arab summit meeting at Tā^cif repudiated UN Resolution 242, advocated a *jihād* for the delivery of Jerusalem as the capital of a Palestinian state, and extended the Arab boycott of Israel.

       Mar.-Apr.:   Tensions increased along the Israeli-Lebanese border.

       Apr. 1:   Fighting in Zahla, Lebanon; beginning of Syrian-Israeli "missile crises."

       Jun. 7:   Israeli aircraft destroyed an Iraqi nuclear reactor near Baghdad.

       Jun.17-19:   Large-scale clashes in Egypt between Muslims and Christians.

       Jun. 21:   Banī-Ṣadr, President of Iran, formally stripped of office by *majlis*.

       Jun. 28:   IRP headquarters in Tehran bombed; victims included Ayatollāh Bihishti [Beheshti].

       Jun. 30:   Likud Party, under Menachem Begin, won Israeli election.

       Jul. 28:   Banī-Ṣadr, ex-President, and Mas^cūd Rajavī, head of Mujahidīn-i Khalq, fled Iran to Europe.

       Aug. 8:   Fahd's Eight-Point Plan for Peace in the Middle East presented.

       Oct. 6:   Anwar al-Sādāt assassinated.

       Oct. 6:   Ḥusnī Mubārak became President of Egypt.

       Oct. 29:   U.S. Senate upheld sale of AWACs to Saudi Arabia.

       Nov.:   Israeli Knesset made Israeli laws applicable to the Golan Heights.

       Nov. 25:   Arab summit meeting at Fez rejected Fahd's peace plan.

1982   Apr. 25:   Israel completed withdrawal from the Sinai Peninsula.

       Jun. 13:   King Khālid of Saudi Arabia died; replaced by Crown Prince Fahd. Abdullāh became Crown Prince.

       Jun. 6:   Israelis invaded Lebanon, which they called "Operation Peace for Northern Galilee."

       Aug. 21:   PLO began evacuation from Beirut.

       Aug. 23:   Bashīr al-Jumayyil [Gemayel] became President-Elect of Lebanon.

       Aug. 25:   U.S. Marines arrived in Beirut port area, followed by French and Italian troops. They left September 10.

       Sep. 1:   U.S. President, Ronald Reagan, presented peace plan for Middle East.

       Sep.5-8:   Fez Peace Plan proposed at Arab summit meeting.

       Sep. 14:   Bashīr al-Jumayyil [Gemayel] President-Elect of Lebanon, assassinated.

       Sep.16-18:   Massacres in Sabra and Shatila Palestinian refugee camps by Christian Phalangists.

       Sep. 21:   Amīn al-Jumayyil [Gemayel] elected President of Lebanon.

       Sep. 25:   Large-scale political demonstration in Tel Aviv that called for inquiry into Beirut massacres.

       Sep. 27:   French, Italian and, on the 29th, U.S. troops returned to Beirut.

       Sep. 28:   Kahan Commission established in Israel to investigate Sabra and Shatila massacres.

       Nov. 9:   Kenan Evren elected as 7th President of Turkey after referendum on new Constitution on November 7th.

1983   Feb. 8:   Report given by Israeli Kahan Commission on Beirut massacres.

       May 7:   Revolt within al-Fatah against ^cArafāt leadership, led by Abū Mūsā [Mūsā Sa^cīd].

       May 27:   Agreement between Israel and Lebanon for withdrawal of foreign troops from Lebanon.

1983   Sep. 14:   Israelis withdrew from Central
                   Lebanon to Awali River.

        Sep. 15:   Begin submitted his resignation
                   as Israel's Prime Minister. Yitzhak
                   Shamir replaced Begin as head of Herut
                   political party.

        Oct. 10:   Shamir was confirmed by Knesset
                   as Prime Minister.

        Oct. 23:   American and French forces in
                   Lebanon suffered significant losses
                   from truck bombs.

        Oct. 30:   Lebanese reconciliation meeting
                   in Geneva.

        Nov. 6:   Turgut Özal, head of Motherland
                   Party, was elected Turkish Prime Min-
                   ister.

        Nov. 14:   Turkish Republic of Northern
                   Cyprus declared by Rauf Denktash,
                   Turkish Cypriot leader.

        Nov. 29:   Major U.S.-Israel agreement
                   announced on military cooperation and
                   economic issues.

        Dec. 4:   U.S. bombing raid into Lebanon.

        Dec. 20:   Evacuation of pro-ᶜArafāt Pal-
                   estinians from Tripoli completed.

        Dec. 29:   Sporadic fighting in and around
                   Beirut among numerous groups continued.

VII. Acronyms of Twentieth-Century Organizations

There is no single, extensive collection of abbreviations dealing with the political, social and economic groups formed in the 20th century. Each new resistance movement, military *junta*, political party, oil company, interstate organization, etc. brings with it a new abbreviation. The easiest way to locate the full name of an undefined abbreviation — which, by context, is connected with 20th-century Southwest Asia and Egypt — is to turn to the index of any of the standard works on the Modern Era, such as:

* Abid A. Al-Marayati (Ed.), *The Middle East: Its Government and Politics* (Belmont, CA: Duxbury Press, 1972); and

* Tareq Y. Ismael, *Governments and Politics of the Contemporary Middle East* (Homewood, IL: The Dorsey Press, 1970).

* Yaacov Shimoni and Evyatar Levine (Eds.), *Political Dictionary of the Middle East in the Twentieth Century* (New York: Quadrangle [The New York Times Book Co.; rev. ed.], 1974), does not list groups by abbreviations.

* Clio Dictionaries in Political Science has announced L. Zering, *The Middle East Political Dictionary*, as Volume 5 of their series, and it may be helpful.

ADF   <u>Arab Deterrent Force</u> [1976-]: The multinational, Syrian-dominated Arab force sent in 1976 into Lebanon to end the internal strife.

AIOC   <u>Anglo-Iranian Oil Co.</u> [1935-51]: British-controlled oil company; superseded APOC.

AL   <u>Arab League</u> [1945-]: Members, as of 1983, were Algeria, Bahrain, Egypt, Iraq, Jordan, Kuwait, Lebanon, Libya, Morocco, Qatar, Saudi Arabia, South Yemen, Sudan, Syria, Tunisia, United Arab Emirates, Yemen, Oman, Somalia, Mauritania, and the PLO. Also known as League of Arab States.

ALESCO   <u>Arab League Educational, Cultural and Scientific Organization</u> [1970-]: Its divisions include education, social sciences, humanities and culture, science, documentation and information, and the Institute of Arab Manuscripts.

ALF   <u>Arab Liberation Front</u> [1969-]: A Palestinian *fidā'īyīn* group sponsored by Iraq.

ANM   <u>Arab Nationalist Movement</u> [1950s-]: An Arab, particularly Palestinian, group dominated by George Habash. Precursor to PFLP.

APOC   <u>Anglo-Persian Oil Co.</u> [1930-35]: Earliest Western oil company in the area.

ARAMCO   <u>Arabian-American Oil Co.</u> [1946-]: Owned by Standard Oil of California, Standard Oil of New Jersey, Mobil Oil and Texaco Oil.

ARE   <u>Arab Republic of Egypt</u> [1971-]: Official name of Egypt.

ASU   <u>Arab Socialist Union</u> [1962-]: The only

	legal Egyptian political party.
BP	British Petroleum [1951-]: Superseded AIOC.
CENTO	Central Treaty Organization [1958-]: Members, as of 1976, were Britain, Iran, Pakistan and Turkey. Previously called Baghdad Pact [1955-58] and included Iraq.
CUP	Committee of Union and Progress [1908-18]: Known as "Young Turks." This group of Turkish military leaders ran the Ottoman government and reinstated the 1876 Constitution.
DFLP	Democratic Front for Liberation of Palestine [1969-]: Radical Palestinian fidā'īyīn group founded by Nayif Hawatmeh. Broke off from PFLP. Formerly Popular Democratic Front for Liberation of Palestine [PDFLP].
DP	Democratic Party [1946-60]: A Turkish political party during first republic, dominated by Adnan Menderes, and was in power from 1950 to 1960.
EGPC	Egyptian General Petroleum Co. [1960-]: Egyptian national oil company.
FLOSY	Front for Liberation of Occupied South Yemen [1966-67]: Radical group opposed to British occupation of Aden and South Yemen.
GCC	Gulf Cooperation Council [1981-]: Saudi Arabia, Kuwait, Bahrain, Qatar and UAE joined a regional economic and defense pact on March 10, 1981.
GE	Gush Emmunim ["Group of those who keep faith"; 1973-]: An Israeli pressure group, begun after 1973 elections, whose program includes an active settlement policy in a Greater Israel.

IBRD	International Bank for Reconstruction and Development [1944-]: Created to provide and facilitate international investments.
IDF	Israel Defense Forces [1948-]: Official name for Israeli military forces.
INOC	Iraq National Oil Co. [1958-]: Iraqi national oil company.
IPC	Iraq Petroleum Co. [1929-58]: Composed of APOC [BP], Shell Oil, Compagnie Française, Standard Oil of New Jersey, Mobil Oil and Gulbenkian interests in oil consortium. Superseded TPC.
IRP	Islamic Republican Party, Iran [1979-]: Dominates majlis, judicial system and cabinet.
JNF	Jewish National Fund [Keren Kayemeth; 1901-]: Concerned with fund-raising and acquisition of land in Palestine, and then Israel, for Jewish people.
JP	Justice Party [1961-81]: A major Turkish political party in the 2nd Turkish republic, led by Süleymān Demirel.
KNPC	Kuwait National Petroleum Co. [1960-]: National oil company financed by State of Kuwait.
KOC	Kuwait Oil Co. [1933-]: Western oil consortium of APOC [BP] and Gulf Oil Corporation.
MEPL	Middle East Pipeline, Ltd. [1947]: A company controlled by the AIOC and American oil companies who sought to build a pipeline from Iran to the Mediterranean, but failed.
MFO	Multinational Force and Observers [1981-]: An international force—U.S., Fiji, Colombia, Great Britain, France, Italy, Australia and New Zealand—supervising Treaty of Peace between Egypt and Israel on the Sinai. It replaced UNEF II.

NATO   North Atlantic Treaty Organization [1949-].

NF   National Front [1951-53]: A nationalist Iranian political group dominated by Mosaddeq.

NF   National Front [1964-]: A major, radical political party in South Yemen.

NIOC   National Iranian Oil Company [1951-]: Iranian national oil company.

NLF   National Liberation Front [1954-64]: A radical, anti-British political party in Aden. Later became only legal party of PDRY, the British having transferred power to them.

NSC   National Security Council [Turkish; 1980-]: Military leadership under Kenan Evren, which ran Turkey from *coup* of September 12, 1980.

NUC   National Unity Committee [1961-62]: The military group that ran Turkey for the period between the two republics.

OAPEC   Organization of Arab Petroleum Exporting Countries [1968-]: Membership, as of 1982, was Algeria, Bahrain, Egypt (suspended '79), Iraq, Kuwait, SA, Syria, Tunisia, Libya, Qatar, UAE.

OAU   Organization of African Unity [1963-]: Organization of African states, excluding European-controlled areas, to further African unity and solidarity.

OPEC   Organization of Petroleum Exporting Countries [1960-]: Membership, as of 1982, was Algeria, Ecuador, Iran, Iraq, Indonesia, Gabon, Kuwait, Libya, Nigeria, Qatar, Saudi Arabia, Venezuela and UAE.

PDFLP   See DFLP above.

PDRY   People's Democratic Republic of Yemen [1970-]: The official name for the government of South Yemen. From 1967-70, it was known as PRSY [People's Republic of South Yemen].

PFLO   Popular Front for the Liberation of Oman [1974-]: A group opposed to the ex-isting government of Oman. Formerly PFLOAG.

PFLOAG   Popular Front for Liberation of Oman and the Arabian Gulf [1968-74]: A group opposed to the existing governments of Oman, UAE and other Gulf states sponsored by the PDRY.

PFLP   Popular Front for Liberation of Palestine [1968-]: Marxist Palestinian *fidā'īyīn* group founded by George Habash.

PFLP-GC   Popular Front for Liberation of Palestine - General Command [1968-]: A radical Palestinian *fidā'īyīn* group founded by Aḥmad Jibrīl. Later broke off from PFLP.

PLA   Palestine Liberation Army [1964-]: The official army of the PLO.

PLF   Palestine Liberation Front [1965?-68]: A Palestinian *fidā'īyīn* group founded by Aḥmad Jibrīl. Later merged with part of ANM and other groups to form PFLP.

PLO   Palestine Liberation Organization [1964-]: Umbrella organization of various Palestinian groups.

PNC   Palestine National Council [1965-]: Established in 1965 with 182 members. In 1977 it increased to 292.

POLP   Popular Organization for Liberation of Palestine [1969-]: Maoist Palestinian *fidā'īyīn* group.

PPS   Parti Populaire Syrien [1932-]: Syrian national party founded by Anṭun Saᶜada. Also known as SSNP.

PSP   Progressive Socialist Party [1949-]: A major Lebanese Druze political party associated with Kamāl Jumblāṭ.

RCC   Revolutionary Command Council [1952-56]: Egyptian military group, led by Gamāl ᶜAbd al-Nāṣir, which planned the 1952 *coup* and then ran the government under leadership of Muḥammad Naguib.

RPP   Republican People's Party [1923-81]: A

	major Turkish political party founded by Muṣṭafā Kemal Atatürk.
SAR	Syrian Arab Republic [1961-]: Official name of Syria.
SAVAK	Sāzeman-e Attil^cāt va Amniyat-e Keshvar [Organization for the information and security of the country]: Iranian security forces combine the roles of the FBI and CIA.
SSNP	Syrian Social Nationalist Party: See PPS.
TAPline	Trans-Arabian Pipeline Co. [1947-]: A subsidiary of Aramco that built a 1,068.2-mile pipeline from Saudi Arabia to Sidon.
TPC	Turkish Petroleum Co. [1912-29]: Western-dominated oil company that became basis for IPC.
UAA	Union of Arab Amirates: Also known as UAE [United Arab Emirates].
UAE	Union of Arab Emirates [1971-]: Members, as of 1974, include: Abu Dhabi, Dubai, Sharjah, Ahman, Umm al-Qaywayn, al-Fujayrah and Ras al-Khaymah [also United Arab Emirates].
UAR	United Arab Republic [1958-61]: Union of Egypt and Syria, with the former keeping the name until 1971, when it became the ARE.
UJA	United Jewish Appeal: A major, pro-Israeli Jewish fund-raising group in the United States.
UNCC	United Nations Conciliation Commission [1948-49]: Commission composed of France, Turkey and U.S. It aimed to achieve a peace settlement between Israel and the Arab States.
UNDOF	United Nations Disengagement Observer Force [1974-]: An international military force established in June 1974 to patrol the buffer region separating Israeli and Syrian forces on the Golan Heights.
UNEF	United Nations Emergency Force [1957-67; 1974-79]: An international military force established after the 1956 Suez War between Egypt and Israel and re-activated after the 1973 War.
UNEF II	See UNEF. Re-established UNEF after 1973 War.
UNESCO	United Nations Educational, Scientific and Cultural Organization.
UNGA	United Nations General Assembly.
UNIFIL	United Nations Interim Force in Lebanon [1978-]: Established after March 1978, when Israel initiated military actions in southern Lebanon.
UNMAC	United Nations Mixed Armistice Commission [1949-]: International groups to supervise and investigate truce violations between Egypt and Israel [UNEIMAC], Jordan and Israel [UNJIMAC], Syria and Israel [UNSIMAC], and Lebanon and Israel [UNLIMAC].
UNOGIL	United Nations Observer Group in Lebanon [1958]: International group to investigate possible Syrian interference during Lebanese Civil War.
UNRPR	United Nations Relief for Palestinian Refugees [1948-49]: Established to provide immediate relief for Palestinian refugees; superseded by UNRWA.
UNRWA	United Nations Relief and Works Agency [1949-]: International group to feed, house and train Palestinian refugees temporarily.
UNSCOP	United Nations Special Committee on Palestine [1947]: UN committee whose majority recommended partition of Palestine.
UNTSO	United Nations Truce Supervision Organization [1948-49]: Established to supervise the Arab-Israeli armistice.
UNYOM	United Nations Yemen Observation Mission [1963-64]: A small international force to oversee the truce in the Yemen Civil War. Unsuccessful and was withdrawn after 15 months.

WZO   <u>World Zionist Organization</u> [1897-]: A
_____   major Zionist body.

YAR   <u>Yemen Arab Republic</u> [1962-]: Official
               name of Northern Yemen.

VIII. Historical Atlas

The lack of an adequate historical atlas has been a major lacuna in Islamic studies. Dr. R. Roolvink and others compiled the *Historical Atlas of the Muslim Peoples* (Amsterdam: Djambatan, 1957), which has almost 50 multicolored maps covering the area from Spain to Indonesia, and from the pre-Islamic period to the 20th century. Many of them concentrate on particular areas and specific chronological periods. However, the lack of an index is a serious weakness.

But the weakness of Roolvink's work is the strength of Harry W. Hazard's *Atlas of Islamic History*, 3rd ed. (Princeton: Princeton University Press, 1954). His index is not only thorough, but, in many cases, includes the Arabic, Persian, Ottoman and European spellings of a place's name. Each map is accompanied by a list of the dynasties and their dates for all the areas covered. The weakness is in the maps. The first 13 out of 18 cover a fixed area: Spain through Iran, and each deals with a century of changes. They are, therefore, limited in detail and each covers a very long chronological period.

A work limited to the Arab world, from Iraq and Arabia through Spain, is Rolf Reichert's *A Historical and Regional Atlas of the Arab World, [Maps and Chronological Survey]*, (Rio de Janeiro: Sedegra Sociedade Editora e Grafica, Ltd., 1969), in English and Portuguese. The 60 black-and-white maps of fair quality cover the Arabian Peninsula, Syria and Mesopotamia, Northeast Africa and Northwest Africa (Maghrib), on a century-by-century basis. Each map is accompanied by a text covering the major historical events, as well as six genealogy tables. An index is lacking.

An example of an excellent historical atlas is the *Historical Atlas of Iran*, published by Tehran University in 1971, under the editorship of Seyyid Hossein Nasr, Ahmad Mostofi and Abbās Zaryab. Of the very large, colored maps, 20 are of use for students of Islamic Iran. Each map, with locations in Persian and English/French, includes all the major cities, many minor ones, general political lines, provinces and bodies of water. Each map is accompanied by a brief historical survey in Persian, French and English. All locations are indexed.

Another specialized publication is the posthumous work of Donald E. Pitcher: *An Historical Geography of the Ottoman Empire from Earliest Times to the End of the Sixteenth Century* (Leiden: E.J. Brill, 1972). As the title indicates, the 36 multicolored maps cover the years from the rise of the Ottomans to 1612. The political and provincial divisions are given in great detail. This work also includes an historical survey which stresses the dates of the territorial acquisitions and an index.

In the decade since the first edition of *A Near East Studies Handbook* was prepared, a number of atlases have appeared or have been announced, which will alleviate many of the problems facing those needing historical atlases. The almost 60 maps in William C. Brice, ed., *An Historical Atlas of Islam* (Leiden: E.J. Brill, 1981), cover the Islamic world from the Atlantic to the Philippines. Each map, in color, gives a sense of the topography and identifies major geographical features. These maps are best for indicating military campaigns, trade routes, and general political boundaries. There are maps of Mecca [Makka], Medina [al-Madīna] and Istanbul, which are very helpful. There is also an index.

Francis Robinson, *Atlas of the Islamic World Since 1500* (New York: Facts on File, Inc., 1982), is an excellent, extensive essay on Islamic political, cultural and religious history with magnificent photographs. The well-drawn, colored maps — limited in number — are outstanding and are particularly valuable for religious developments. There is an index. Unfortunately, the same high praise cannot be given for *Atlas of the Arab World*, compiled by Michael Dempsey (New York: Facts on File, Inc., 1983), whose maps are brightly colored, but give only the most general economic and political information.

Throughout Marshall G.S. Hodgson, *The Venture of Islam*, 3 vols. (Chicago: University of Chicago Press, 1974), there are black-and-white maps reflecting political developments throughout the Islamic world. As with the Robinson book, they supplement the text and are not the focus of the work. There is no index for the maps.

The finest historical atlas is being prepared by the German Research Council and the University of Tübingen. It is *Tübingen Atlas des Vorderen Orients* [*TAVO*], (Wiesbaden: Dr. Ludwig Reichert Verlag, 1977-). This atlas is being produced in large, unbound sheets measuring approximately 20" by 28" which, when finished, should number over 300 sheets. One-third of the series will be on physical geography, including climate, vegetation, population, etc. The historical maps go from the Stone Age to the Modern Age, and will include detailed maps of Islamic cities, locations of major religious movements, etc. An excellent review of this work was written by Michael Bonine in the *MESA Bulletin*, XVII.1 (July 1983):103-105.

Computer-generated maps are being developed for classroom use and could be on the market in the near future. Justin McCarthy, Department of History (University of Louisville), has developed one system that can be adjusted to meet the needs of a particular teacher. Herbert Bodman, Department of History (University of North Carolina), is editing a massive, computer-generated historical atlas entitled *Atlas of the Islamic Peoples*, which is being funded in part by a grant from the National Endowment for the Humanities. It should be available in 1986.

It is also possible for individuals to produce their own computer-generated maps, using the World Data Bank II, a data base of the world's coastlines, developed by the Central Intelligence Agency and now distributed by the National Technical Information Service. The data base includes islands, lakes, rivers, canals and international political boundaries. It is also possible to mark the locations of cities by including their coordinates.

More surprising than some of the inadequacies of the historical atlases for the pre-1900 period is the lack of a good collection dealing with 20th-century political histories. Over half the maps in this book reflect proposed and actual divisions of the Middle East for this century because they are not readily available elsewhere.

For a fuller discussion of all of these resources, the reader may consult Gerry A. Hale's "Maps and Atlases of the Middle East," *MESA Bulletin*, III.3 (October 1969):17-39. The Hale survey is being updated by Douglas L. Johnson, Mary A. Powers, and Charlotte A. Slocum of Clark University, in a 1984 edition of the *MESA Bulletin*.

Cost has been the major factor for limiting the number of maps included within this atlas — a number which could easily have been doubled under somewhat less inflationary circumstances. The Muslim conquests and political changes in North Africa and Spain have not been included in order to be consistent with the geographical limits of this book. The spellings of place names have usually followed the accepted English form rather than a transliterated one; e.g.: Aleppo for Ḥalab, although the index includes these transliterated forms as cross-references. As indicated in the Introduction, line drawings have been used for financial reasons.

1. EGYPT AND SOUTHWEST ASIA, PHYSICAL CHARACTERISTICS

2. CITIES OF TURKEY

3. CITIES OF LEBANON AND WESTERN SYRIA

4. CITIES OF ISRAEL, GAZA, WEST BANK, AND WESTERN JORDAN

5. CITIES OF IRAQ

6. CITIES OF IRAN

7. CITIES OF EGYPT

8. EGYPT AND SOUTHWEST ASIA, CIRCA 600

9. CONQUESTS, RĀSHIDŪN AND ʿUMAYYAD PERIODS

10. MEDIEVAL BAGHDAD AND IRAQ

Based on Le Strange

11. ʿABBĀSID PROVINCES

12.   SYRIAN PROVINCES, ᶜABBĀSID PERIOD

13. EGYPT AND SOUTHWEST ASIA, LATE 9th CENTURY

14. EGYPT AND SOUTHWEST ASIA, EARLY 10th CENTURY

15. EGYPT AND SOUTHWEST ASIA, LATE 10th CENTURY

16. EGYPT AND SOUTHWEST ASIA, LATE 11th CENTURY

Seljuk Sultanate of Rūm

Principality of Armenia

Tarsus

County of Edessa

Edessa

TIGRIS R.

R. of Antioch

Aleppo

Antioch

Latakia

Raqqa

EUPHRATES R.

Shayzar

Cyprus

Hisn al-Akrad

C. of Tripoli

Hims

Tripoli

MEDITERRANEAN SEA

Beirut

Sidon

Tyre

Damascus

Kingdom of Jerusalem

Acre

Caesarea

JORDAN R.

Jaffa

Nablus

Jerusalem

Ascalon

Gaza

DEAD SEA

Karak

Al-Arish

Farama

Montreal

Qulzum

Fāṭimid Caliphate

RED SEA

0   50   100
MILES

17. CRUSADING STATES, CIRCA 1130

18. EGYPT AND SOUTHWEST ASIA, LATE 12th CENTURY

Imbādah

Border of the Nile 800 A.D.

Present border of the Nile

Al-Maqs
(Umm Dunaym)

Canal to Red Sea

Fāṭimid City
(969)

Duqqi

NILE RIVER

Muqaṭṭam
Spur

Mosque of
c Ibn
Al-   Tūlūn
Qaṭā'i   (879)
(870)

Citadel (1176)

Port of
Fustāt

Al-ʿAskar
(750)

Rawḍah

Mosque of
ʿAmr
c
Jīzah   Fustat
(640)
Babylon

19. MEDIEVAL FUSTAT (CAIRO)
Based on Abu Lughod

20. EGYPT AND SOUTHWEST ASIA, EARLY 14th CENTURY

21. EGYPT AND SOUTHWEST ASIA, LATE 14th CENTURY

22. OTTOMAN CONQUESTS TO 1451

23. EGYPT AND SOUTHWEST ASIA, LATE 15th CENTURY

24. OTTOMAN EMPIRE IN EUROPE AND ANATOLIA, 1451-1683

1. SELIM MOSQUE
2. MEHMED MOSQUE
3. SULEIMAN MOSQUE
4. BAYAZID MOSQUE
5. NEW MOSQUE
6. SERAI
7. HAGIA SOPHIA
8. AHMED MOSQUE

25. ISTANBUL

26. EGYPT AND SOUTHWEST ASIA, 17th CENTURY

27. OTTOMAN EMPIRE IN EUROPE AND ANATOLIA, 1683-1923

28.   EGYPT AND SOUTHWEST ASIA, CIRCA 1914

29.   THE SYKES-PICOT AGREEMENT, 1916

① International Zone by Treaty of Sèvres.

② Greek Zone by W.W. I promises.

③ Italian Zone by W.W. I promises and Treaty of Sèvres.

④ French Zone by W.W. I promises and Treaty of Sèvres.

⑤ Frontier by Treaty of Sèvres.

⑥ Russian Zone by Constantinople Agreement, then Armenian by Treaty of Sèvres.

⑦ Free Port.

⑧ Russian Zone by Constantinople Agreement.

30.   ALLIED PLANS FOR TURKEY, 1915-1920

31.   THE SAN REMO AGREEMENT

32.   SYRIAN AND LEBANESE PROVINCES DURING FRENCH MANDATE

33.   SYRIAN ADMINISTRATIVE PROVINCES, POST WWII

34. THE PEEL COMMISSION PARTITION PLAN, 1937

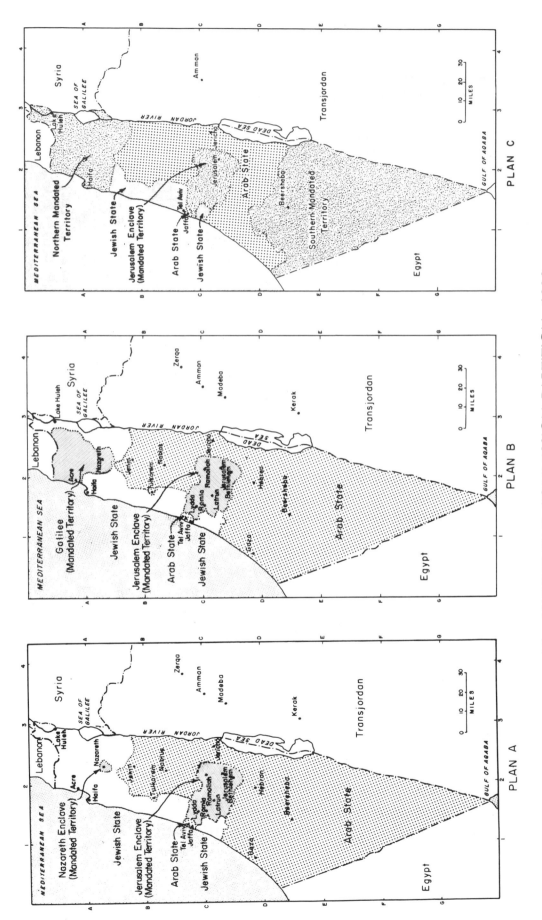

35. WOODHEAD COMMISSION PARTITION, 1939

36.   MORRISON-GRADY PARTITION PLAN, 1946

37.   U.N. PARTITION PLAN, NOVEMBER 29, 1967

38.   THE ISRAELI-ARAB ARMISTICE LINES, 1949

40. IRANIAN PROVINCES, POST WWII

39. PROPOSED DIVISIONS OF IRAN, 1907-46

41. EGYPT AND SOUTHWEST ASIA, 1960

42.   EGYPT AND SUDAN

43. ISRAEL AND OCCUPIED LANDS, 1967

44. ARAB-ISRAELI DISPUTE, 1973-74

45. ARABIAN PENINSULA, 1974

Mediterranean Sea

Port Sa'id

Al-'Arish

Beersheba

Qantara

ISRAEL

Isma'ilyya

I
2 MONTHS

Interim Phase Disengagement Line

Al-'Arish

V

9 MONTHS

Suez

EGYPT

Ra's

Muhammad Line

JORDAN

Al-Sudr

Eilat

5 MONTHS

III

Abū
Zunayma

Abū Rudays

II

3 MONTHS

Gulf of 'Aqaba

SAUDI ARABIA

Gulf of Suez

St. Catherine

V 9 MONTHS

IV
7
MONTHS

Al-Tūr

50 MILES

0   50 KM

– – – The 1949 Armistice Line

– · – International Boundary

· · · · · The 1975 Disengagement Lines

– – – – Egyptian advance-line during subphases of interim withdrawal

· · · · · · Israeli withdrawal-line during subphases of interim withdrawal

Red Sea

Sharm al-Shaykh

Ra's Muhammad

46.   EGYPTIAN-ISRAELI DISENGAGEMENT AGREEMENT, 1975

47. EGYPTIAN-ISRAELI PEACE AGREEMENT

48. LEBANON, 1976   49. BEIRUT, 1983

50. PROVINCES OF LEBANON

51.   JERUSALEM

IX. Gazetteer

Data for this Gazetteer were gathered from a number of sources, the most important of which are listed below. While there was an agreement on the longitudinal and latitudinal co-ordinates for each of the cities, there was no agreement on the estimated populations. Thus, population figures should be used with great caution and should be treated as reflecting a general level or order of magnitude. For those cities where population figures were not available, a "*" has been placed after their names.

* *1981 Commercial Atlas and Marketing Guide* (Chicago: Rand McNally & Co., 1981).

* *The Times Atlas of the World* (Boston: Houghton Mifflin Co., 1967).

* John Paxton, ed. *The Statesman's Year-Book, 1982-1983* (New York: St. Martin's Press, 1982).

* *Webster's New Geographical Dictionary* (Springfield, MA: G & C Merriam Co., 1980).

* *Middle East and North Africa, 1982-1983.* 29th ed. (London: Europa Publications, Ltd., 1982).

* *Rand McNally's World Atlas, Census* (Chicago: Rand McNally & Co., 1981).

Abadan, Iran [Ābādān]:	Pop.: 296,081 (1976) 31° 06' N; 52° 40' E	Antalya, Turkey:	Pop.: 173,501 (1980) 36° 53' N; 30° 42' E
Abu Dhabi, UAE [Abū Zaby]:	50,000 (1968) 24° 28' N; 54° 25' E	Antioch, Turkey [Antakya, Anṭākiyah]:	66,520 (1970) 36° 12' N; 36° 10' E
Acre, Israel [ᶜAkko]:	37,900 (1979) 32° 55' N; 35° 04' E	Aqaba, Jordan [al-ᶜAqabah]:	26,986 (1979) 30° 08' N; 43° 40' E
Adana, Turkey:	574,515 (1980) 37° 00' N; 35° 19' E	Ardebil, Iran [Ardabīl]:	147,404 (1976) 38° 15' N; 48° 18' E
Aden, PDRY [South Yemen]:	264,326 (1973) 12° 47' N; 45° 03' E	al-Arish, Egypt [al-ᶜArīsh]:	40,388 (1966) 31° 08' N; 33° 48' E
Ahwaz, Iran [Ahvaz]:	329,006 (1976) 31° 17' N; 48° 43' E	Ascalon, Israel [Ashqelon, al-ᶜAshqalān]:	40,338 (1976) 31° 40' N; 34° 35' E
Aleppo, Syria [Halab]:	639,326 (1970) 36° 14' N; 37° 10' E	Aswan, Egypt [Aswān]:	144,654 (1976) 24° 05' N; 32° 56' E
Alexandretta, Turkey [Iskenderun]:	72,297 (1970) 36° 37' N; 36° 08' E	Asyut, Egypt [Asyūt]:	213,751 (1976) 27° 14' N; 31° 07' E
Alexandria, Egypt [al-Iskandariyah]:	2,317,705 (1976) 31° 13' N; 29° 55' E		
Amman, Jordan [ᶜAmmān]:	648,587 (1979) 31° 57' N; 35° 56' E	Baalbek, Lebanon [Baᶜlabakk]:	16,000 (1970) 34° 00' N; 35° 55' E
Ankara, Turkey:	1,877,755 (1980) 39° 55' N; 32° 50' E	Baghdad, Iraq:	1,300,000 (1970) 32° 20' N; 44° 26' E

---

* = Population figure not available.

Bandar Abbas, Iran [Bandar ʿAbbās]:	Pop.: 89,103 (1976) 27° 12' N; 56° 15' E	Hilla, Iraq [al-Hillah]:	Pop.: 128,000 (1970) 32° 30' N; 44° 24' E
Baniyas, Syria [Bānyās]:	* 35° 12' N; 35° 57' E	Hodeida, Yemen [al-Hudaydah]:	126,386 (1980) 14° 50' N; 42° 38' E
Basra, Iraq [al-Baṣrah]:	370,900 (1970) 30° 30' N; 47° 50' E	Homs, Syria [Ḥimṣ]:	215,423 (1970) 34° 44' N; 36° 43' E
Beersheba, Israel [Be'er Sheva]:	109,600 (1981) 31° 15' N; 34° 77' E		
Beirut, Lebanon [Bayrut]:	800,000 (1972) 33° 52' N; 35° 31' E	Irbid, Jordan:	113,000 (1973) 32° 33' N; 35° 51' E
Bursa, Turkey:	445,113 (1980) 40° 12' N; 29° 04' E	Isfahan, Iran [Esfahan]:	671,825 (1976) 32° 41' N; 51° 41' E
Bushire, Iran [Bushehr, Bushehir]:	* 28° 59' N; 50° 51' E	Ismailia, Egypt [al-Ismāʿīliyah]:	145,930 (1976) 30° 36' N; 32° 15' E
		Istanbul, Turkey:	2,772,708 (1980) 41° 02' N; 28° 57' E
Cairo, Egypt [al-Qāhirah]:	8,539,000 (1979) 30° 03' N; 31° 15' E	Izmir, Turkey [Smyrna]:	757,854 (1980) 38° 25' N; 27° 10' E
		Izmit, Turkey [Ismid, Nicomedia]:	164,675 (1979) 40° 27' N; 29° 43' E
Damascus, Syria [Dimashq]:	836,668 (1970) 33° 30' N; 35° 31' E		
Damietta, Egypt [Dumyāt]:	86,327 (1966) 31° 26' N; 31° 48' E	Jaffa, Israel [Yaffo][with Tel Aviv population]:	334,900 (1981) 32° 05' N; 34° 46' E
Dhahran, Saudi Arabia [al-Ẓahrān]:	22,500 (1965) 26° 18' N; 50° 05' E	Jedda, Saudi Arabia [Jiddah]:	561,104 (1974) 21° 30' N; 39° 10' E
Diyarbakir, Turkey [Diyarbakr]:	235,617 (1980) 37° 55' N; 40° 14' E	Jericho, West Bank [Arīḥā]:	* 31° 51' N; 35° 27' E
Doha, Qatar [al-Dawhah]:	80,000 (1980) 25° 15' N; 51° 36' E	Jerusalem, Israel [Yerushalayim, al-Quds]:	407,100 (1981) 31° 47' N; 35° 13' E
Dubai, UAE [Dubayy]:	60,000 (1968) 25° 14' N; 55° 17' E		
		Karbalā', Iraq:	107,500 (1970) 32° 37' N; 44° 03' E
Edirne, Turkey:	53,806 (1970) 41° 40' N; 26° 34' E	Kāshān, Iran:	84,545 (1976) 33° 59' N; 51° 35' E
Eilat, Israel [Elat, Elath]:	12,800 (1972) 29° 33' N; 34° 57' E	Kermān, Iran:	140,309 (1976) 30° 18' N; 57° 05' E
Erzurum, Turkey [Erzerum]:	190,241 (1980) 39° 57' N; 41° 17' E	Kermānshāh, Iran:	290,861 (1976) 34° 19' N; 47° 04' E
		Khartoum, Sudan [al-Khurtūm]:	333,921 (1973) 15° 33' N; 32° 31' E
Gallipoli, Turkey [Gelibolu]:	14,716 (1970) 40° 25' N; 26° 41' E	Kirkūk, Iraq:	207,900 (1970) 35° 26' N; 44° 26' E
Gaza, Gaza Strip [Ghazzah]:	118,272 (1967) 31° 30' N; 34° 28' E	Konya, Turkey:	329,139 (1980) 37° 51' N; 32° 31' E
Haifa, Israel:	230,000 (1981) 32° 49' N; 34° 59' E	Kufa, Iraq [al-Kūfah]:	30,862 (1966) 32° 02' N; 44° 25' E
Hama, Syria [Hamāh]:	137,421 (1970) 35° 09' N; 36° 44' E	Kuwait, Kuwait [al-Kuwait, Kuwayt]:	80,008 (1970) 29° 20' N; 48° 00' E
Hamadān, Iran:	155,846 (1976) 34° 46' N; 48° 35' E		
Hebron, West Bank [al-Khalīl]:	38,348 (1973) 31° 32' N; 35° 06' E	Latakia, Syria [al-Lādhiqiyah]:	125,716 (1970) 35° 31' N; 35° 47' E
Helwan, Egypt [Ḥulwān]:	* 29° 51' N; 31° 20' E	Luxor, Egypt [al-Uqsur, al-Qusur]:	77,578 (1966) 25° 41' N; 32° 24' E

Ma'an, Jordan:	Pop.: 9,500 (1973)	30° 11' N; 35° 45' E
Malatya, Turkey:	179,074 (1980)	38° 22' N; 38° 18' E
Mansura, Egypt [al-Manṣurah]:	259,387 (1976)	31° 03' N; 31° 23' E
Mardin, Turkey:	33,740 (1980)	37° 19'N; 40° 43' E
Mecca, Saudi Arabia [Makkah]:	366,807 (1974)	21° 26' N; 39° 49' E
Medina, Saudi Arabia [al-Madīnah]:	198,186 (1974)	24° 31' N; 39° 35' E
Meshed, Iran [Mashhad]:	670,180 (1976)	36° 16' N; 59° 34' E
al-Minya, Egypt:	146,423 (1966)	28° 06' N; 30° 45' E
Mosul, Iraq [al-Mawṣil]:	293,100 (1970)	36° 21' N; 43° 08' E
Muscat, Oman [Masqat]:	50,000 (1981)	23° 37' N; 58° 38' E

Nablus, West Bank [Nābulus]:	44,223 (1978)	32° 13' N; 35° 16' E
al-Najaf, Iraq:	179,200 (1970)	31° 59' N; 44° 19' E
Najrān, Saudi Arabia:	47,501 (1974)	17° 31' N; 44° 19' E
Nazareth, Israel [Nazerat]:	33,300 (1972)	32° 42' N; 35° 18' E

Omdurman, Sudan [Umm Durmān]:	299,401 (1973)	15° 37' N; 30° 29' E

Port Fuad, Egypt [Būr Fuᶜad]:	*	31° 16' N; 32° 19' E
Port Said, Egypt [Būr Saᶜīd]:	282,977 (1966)	31° 17' N; 32° 18' E
Port Sudan, Sudan [Būr Sūdān]:	132,631 (1973)	19° 38' N; 37° 07' E
Port Taufiq, Egypt:	*	29° 57' N; 32° 34' E

al-Qanṭara, Egypt:	22,477 (1966)	30° 52' N; 32° 20' E
Qazvīn, Iran [Kazvin]:	138,527 (1976)	36° 16' N; 50° 00' E
Qom, Iran [Qum]:	246,831 (1976)	34° 39' N; 50° 57' E
Quneitra, Syria [al-Qunayṭiraḥ, Kuneitra]:	*	33° 08' N; 35° 49' E
Qusair, Egypt [al-Quṣayr]:	5,525 (1966)	26° 04' N; 34° 15' E

Rafah, Gaza Strip [Rafiah]:	Pop.: 49,800 (1968)	31° 18' N; 34° 15' E
Ramallah, West Bank [Rām Allāh]:	*	31° 55' N; 35° 12' E
Resht, Iran [Rasht]:	187,203 (1976)	37° 18' N; 49° 38' E
Riyadh, Saudi Arabia [al-Riyādh]:	666,840 (1974)	24° 39' N; 46° 46' E
Rosetta, Egypt [Rashīd]:	36,711 (1966)	31° 25' N; 30° 25' E

Safed, Israel [Zefat]:	13,600 (1972)	32° 57' N; 35° 27' E
Sāmarrā', Iraq:	24,746 (1970)	34° 13' N; 43° 52' E
Samsun, Turkey:	198,749 (1980)	41° 17' N; 36° 22' E
Sanᶜā', Yemen:	227,817 (1980)	15° 24' N; 44° 14' E
Sharm al-Shaykh, Egypt [Sharm el-Sheikh]:	*	27° 51' N; 34° 16' E
Shīrāz, Iran:	416,408 (1976)	29° 38' N; 52° 34' E
Sidon, Lebanon [Ṣaydā']:	34,500 (1970)	33° 32' N; 35° 22' E
Sinop, Turkey:	15,096 (1970)	42° 02' N; 35° 09' E
Sivas, Turkey:	172,864 (1980)	39° 44' N; 37° 01' E
Suez, Egypt [al-Suways]:	193,965 (1967)	29° 59' N; 32° 33' E

Taᶜizz, Yemen:	81,000 (1975)	13° 35' N; 44° 02' E
Tabrīz, Iran:	598,576 (1976)	38° 05' N; 46° 18' E
Tabūk, Saudi Arabia [Tabouk]:	74,825 (1974)	28° 22' N; 36° 32' E
Taif, Saudi Arabia [Taᶜif]:	204,857 (1974)	21° 15' N; 40° 21' E
Ṭanṭā, Egypt:	283,240 (1976)	30° 48' N; 31° 00' E
Tehrān, Iran:	4,496,159 (1976)	35° 40' N; 51° 26' E
Tel Aviv, Israel [with Jaffa population]:	334,900 (1981)	32° 05' N; 34° 46' E
Tiberias, Israel [Teverya, Ṭabariyah]:	23,900 (1970)	32° 48' N; 35° 32' E
Trabzon, Turkey [Trebezond]:	80,795 (1970)	41° 00' N; 39° 43' E
Tripoli, Lebanon [Ṭarābulus]:	150,000 (1972)	34° 27' N; 35° 50' E

Tyre, Lebanon [Ṣūr]:   Pop.: 12,500 (1970)
_____   33° 16' N; 35° 12' E

Urfa, Turkey: 100,654 (1970)
_____   37° 08' N; 38° 45' E

Yazd, Iran: 671,825 (1976)
_____   31° 55' N; 54° 22' E

Zagazig, Egypt   202,575 (1976)
   [al-Zagāzīg]:   30° 35' N; 31° 30' E

Zahle, Lebanon [Zaḥlah]:   29,500 (1970)
                              35° 50' N; 35° 55' E

X. Glossary

^cabd
1. Ordinary word for "slave": *ghulām*, *kul* and *mamlūk*.
2. When used with one of the names of Allāh, it means "servant"; e.g., ^cAbd al-Raḥmān.

abū
The *kunya* part of a name when used in a construct: "The father of ..."

adab
Until ^cAbbāsid period, it meant necessary, general culture for gentlemen; later associated with more narrowly defined, specific knowledge needed for a given office or social function. *Belles-lettres*.

ādāt
Customary taxes, authorized by secular law: *kanun*.

adhān
The call to prayer in Arabic by the *muezzin*.

āghā, ağa
Most common usage is as an Ottoman title, usually translated as "chief/senior/master" and used for medium-level and some high-level officials of the Janissary Corps, a sultan's palace service, and local officials. "Sir/gentleman" in Persian. Also applied to eunuchs in the Ottoman palaces.

ahl
"Family/intimates/people/household" or, alone, "wife." Often used in conjunction with other words, as follows:

ahl al-bayt
"The people of the house." Usually means the leading family of an Arabian tribe and, by extension, the Prophet's house.

ahl al-dhimma
ahl al-kitāb
"People of the indefinitely renewed contract"; "People of the Book." Christians and Jews who have a revealed Holy Book and have entered into special relationship with a Muslim community. They are permitted religious freedom in return for payment of the *jizya*.

ahl al-Sunna
"The people of the Sunna" [Sunnī].

akhbār
The term preferred by Shī^cites for *hadīth*.

akhbārīs
The minority Ithnā ^cAsharī Shī^cite legal tradition, which emphasizes reliance on only the *Qur'ān* and *hadīth*.

akıncı
Raider.

aqça, akçe
An Ottoman silver coin of varying weight, fineness and value; known in the West as *aspre* or *asper*.

Alawite
Name given by French and used by Westerners for an extreme Shī^cite group, the Nuṣayrīs, found in modern Syria, who played a critical role in post-1945 Syrian politics. ^c*Alawī* is used by Sunnīs, probably in a pejorative sense.

^cālim [pl. ^culamā']
One learned in the Islamic sciences. Also, a scientist, in modern usage.

aliya
Wave of or period of Jewish immigration to Palestine and Israel, beginning in 1882.

Allāh
God.

^cāmil
"Agent," who could hold various posts, including that of Provin-

	cial Governor; but by 4th/10th century, it usually meant a finance officer, especially in control of the *kharāj*.
amīr, emīr	Originally a military commander. Under the ^CAbbāsids, the title was held by governors and some military commanders. Later used for commander, ruler or prince.
Amīr al-Mu'minīn	"Commander of the Believers." Title adopted by Caliph ^CUmar b. al-Khaṭṭāb and succeeding caliphs.
Amīr al-Umarā'	"Commander of the Commanders." Title granted to powerful military leaders in Baghdad from 324/936.
amṣār [sing. miṣr]	Fortified military camps established by Muslims, such as Fusṭāt, al-Baṣra and al-Kūfa.
al-Anṣār	"The helpers." Term used to designate the Medinans who supported Muḥammad.
^Cārif	"One who knows." Used by *ṣufīs* to contrast their knowledge with that of an *^Cālim*.
^Caql	Legal, systematic reasoning — a source of *sharī^Cah* for Shī^Cites.
^Caṣabīya	Term made famous by historian, Ibn Khaldūn; implies group solidarity, an *esprit de corps*.
Ashkenazim	"Western" Jews—those of European or American origin—primarily those from Eastern Europe and Yiddish-speaking, in contrast to Sephardic Jews [Sephardim].
assassin	Westernized form of *ḥashshāshīn*, one who might have used *hashish*. Applied to medieval Nizārī Shī^Cites of Persia and Syria who used assassination as a weapon.
Assyrian	See Nestorian.
atabeğ, atabey	"Father Prince." A Seljuk term for an advisor and guardian to a Seljuk prince. Some *atabeğs* established their own bases of power and dynastic rule, such as the Zangids.

awqaf	See *waqf*.
a^Cyān	"Notable persons." Originally most important inhabitants of an area; but by 17th century A.D., under Ottomans, it meant local notables with virtual control over their districts; often officially recognized by the Sublime Porte.
^CAyatallāh	A Shī^Cite clergyman who has reached the 3rd level of Shī^Cite higher education, is recognized as a *mujtahid*, and is over 40.
_____	
Bāb-i Āli	See Sublime Porte.
Badawi	See Bedouin.
Bahā'īs	Adherents of a religion founded in 19th-century Persia by Bahā' Allāh and disseminated to Middle East, Europe and the U.S.
bairām	Ottoman term used to refer to the two Muslim festivals: ^CĪd al-Fiṭr and ^CĪd al-Adḥā (see Calendar, p. 9).
banū	Refers to a family/tribe/people when followed by the name of that group's eponymous ancestor.
barīd	"Postal service," specifically the medieval postal and intelligence service.
bast	The sanctuary from secular authority provided by mosques, residences of *^Culamā'*, and other places.
Ba^Cth	"Renaissance/Resurrection." A major Arab Socialist political party founded in Syria, having at various times controlled the governments of Syria and Iran.
bāṭinī	Devotee of esoteric interpretation of sacred texts, particularly associated with Ismā^Cīlīs. The sect appears as *Bāṭinīya* or *Batinites*.
bayt al-māl	Generally refers to a Muslim state treasury, with the *jizya* and *kharāj* as main sources of revenue.

Bedouin — From *badw*. Refers to pastoral no-mads whose language and culture are Arabic.

beğ, bey — Turkish title usually translated as "lord," but also as "chief/master/mister." Found among Turkish peoples or in areas they ruled.

beylerbey — "Bey of Beys." Ottoman title for governor of a province. Title was superseded by *wālī*.

bid^ca — "Innovation." A belief or practice not found in the *sunna* and which the traditionalists consider unacceptable.

_____

caliph, khalīfa — "Successor." Title implied continu-ation by its holder of Muḥammad's leadership over the Muslim com-munity, but without direct, divine revelation.

celali [jelali] — Brigands, military retainers.

Cid — A medieval Spanish form of *sayyid*.

Copt, Qibṭ — A Monophysite Egyptian Christian.

dā^cī — "He who summons." Refers to propa-gandists or missionaries for par-ticular dissenting sects, such as the original ^cAbbāsid movement and the Ismā^cīlīs.

Dār al-Ḥarb — "The Abode of War." Territories not under Muslim political control where *jihādu* take place.

Dār al-Islām — "The Abode of Islam." Territories in which the *sharī^ca* prevails.

dawla — The state or dynasty. Also used as the 2nd part of a *laqab*.

defter, daftar — A register or account book used by administrative officials.

defterdār, daftardār — Keeper of the *defter* (account book); also head of the treasury.

derebey — "Valley lord." Local Anatolian rul-ers who, in the 18th century A.D., were virtually independent of the central Ottoman government.

dervish, — A member of a Muslim mystical order:

dervis/darwīsh — a *ṣūfī*.

devshirme, devşirme — Term for Ottoman system of collect-ing subject Christian boys for training, conversion and even-tual use in palace, Janissary Corps, other government branches.

dhikr — A practice to foster remembering God, usually repeating particular phrases.

dhimmī — See *ahl al-dhimma*.

Dhū-l-Ḥijja — 12th month of Muslim year, in which every Muslim is to make a pil-grimage to Mecca if physically and financially able: *ḥajj*.

Diaspora — Dispersion of Jews from Palestine after Second Temple destroyed in 70 A.D. All Jews outside Israel comprise the Diaspora.

dihqān — Arabized form of Persian term for "head of a village." Historically referred to lower Sassanian feu-dal nobility and descendants under Muslim rule.

dīn — "Religion." Also found as part of a compound *laqab*.

dīnār — Muslim gold coin of varying weight, fineness and value.

dirham — Muslim silver coin of varying weight, fineness and value.

dīwān, divan — 1. Collection of poetry or prose; 2. A register; or 3. A government department.

dragoman — Translator/interpreter. A European-ized form of the Arabic *turjamān*.

Druze — Religious group found chiefly in Greater Syria, whose faith de-rives from Fāṭimid Ismā^cīlī doc-trines and identifies al-Ḥākim as the final Imām.

_____

effendi — Ottoman title of a learned man, a member of a religious or bureau-cratic institution and, later, to numerous military officials and members of an Ottoman family.

	Derived from a Byzantine term for land.
emīr, amīr	See *amīr*.

fals [pl. fulūs]	A copper coin.
falsafa	Philosophy, including natural and moral sciences.
faqīh [pl. fuqahā']	Specialist in *sharīᶜa*, particularly its derivative details; that is, a jurist.
al-Fatah, Fatḥ	Palestinian *fidā'īyīn* group founded by Yāsir ᶜArafāt, which has undertaken operations since 1965.
Fātiḥa	The opening *sūra* of the *Qur'ān*, often used in prayer.
fatwā, fetvā	Opinion on a legal question, issued by a *muftī*.
fallāḥ/fellah [plural: fallāḥin]	"Peasant." Used most often when speaking of Egyptian agricultural population, but applies to any Arab country.
fidā'ī	One who sacrifices himself, especially for his country.
fidā'īyīn, fedayeen	Religious and political organizations in which members risk their lives to achieve their goals. Term is associated with such religious groups as the Assassins; in modern times with various Palestinian organizations.
fiqh	"Jurisprudence," the science of *sharīᶜa*.
firmān, ferman	An Ottoman or Persian imperial rescript or diploma.
fitna	"Rebellion/civil strife," which breaks up the unity of a community.
funduq	"Inn/warehouse/hostel" for foreign merchants, especially Europeans.

gazel	A lyric poem of 4-15 couplets, with the 1st couplet rhyming and the 2nd hemistich rhyming with the hemistich of the 1st couplet.

ghaybah	"Occulation." Refers to the withdrawal of the Shīᶜite Imāms.
ghaybat-i kubra	"Greater Occulation." The period marked by the absence of human intermediaries between the Imām and the faithful, starting with the death of the last *vakil* in 940 and still continuing.
ghāzī	One who takes part in raids against infidels. It later became a title of honor. Muṣṭafā Kemal Atatürk was called *ghāzī*.
ghulām	"Male slave," particularly a military or palace slave.

hadīth	"Tradition." Relates to words or actions of Prophet Muḥammad or his companions. One of four principal sources of the *sharīᶜa* in Sunnī tradition.
ḥāfiz	One who has learned the *Qur'ān* by heart.
Haganah	"Defense." Military arm of the Jewish Agency, which became nucleus for the modern Israeli army.
ḥājib	"Chamberlain." Actual power of an individual with this title varied among medieval Islamic states. In Islamic Spain this office-holder ranked above the *wazīr*.
ḥajj	Formal pilgrimage to Mecca and its environs during particular period in Dhū-l-Ḥijja. Obligatory once in the lifetime of every adult Muslim who is physically and financially able to do so.
ḥājj	Title held by one who has made the "Greater Pilgrimage."
ḥākim	An arbitrator or judge.
han	See *khān*.
Hanafī	Follower of Sunnī *madhhab* or school of law named after Abū Ḥanīfa.
Ḥanbalī	Follower of Sunnī *madhhab* or school of law named after Aḥmad Ibn Ḥanbal.

ḥanīf A pre-Islamic Arab monotheist.

ḥarām "Forbidden," particularly an act prohibited by *sharīᶜa*.

ḥaram "Sanctuary." Associated with particular areas in Mecca and Medina, as well as Jerusalem and Hebron.

ḥarīm/harem Primarily restricted areas of a Muslim's house, particularly the women's quarters.

ḥashīshīya Name given to Syrian followers of Nizārī Ismāᶜīlī Movement.

hijra, hegira "Emigration/departure" of Muḥammad, when he went from Mecca to Medina in 622 A.D. Name is now applied to Muslim calendar that begins in 622 A.D.

ḥisba 1. Functions of one supervising business and public morality, the *muḥtasib*.

2. Duty of every Muslim to fulfill obligations in *sharīᶜa*.

Histadrut General Federation of Labor, founded in Palestine in 1920 by Jewish workers. Involved in traditional trade union activities, cooperative economic ventures, and social/cultural/welfare services.

ᶜĪd al-Adḥā "Sacrificial Feast." Celebrated on 10th of Dhū-l-Ḥijja. Also called al-ᶜĪd al-Kabīr and Büyük Bayram [the Major Festival].

ᶜĪd al-Fiṭr Festival on 1st of Shawwāl, marking end of month of fasting: Ramaḍān. Also called al-ᶜĪd al-Ṣaghīr and Küçük Bayram [the Minor Festival].

idhān The call to prayer.

ijāza Certificate given on completion of a critical text reading, which conveys to recipient (in personal attendance) the authority to expound the text to others.

ijmāᶜ Consensus of a scholarly community of believers on a religious regulation. One of the main sources of the *sharīᶜa*.

ijtihād Use of individual reasoning to determine a specific Islamic rule. Term has shifted meaning over time, varying from very general to extremely restricted applications of personal reasoning.

Ikhwān al-Muslimīn "The Muslim Brethren." Politico-religious movement, founded by Ḥasan al-Bannā' in Egypt in 1926. Stresses fundamentals of Islām as a guide for all activities. Has played important role in modern Egyptian politics and recently gained popularity in other Middle East nations.

ᶜilm "Knowledge," particularly religious or scientific.

iltizām Ottoman system of tax farming, where *iltizām*-holder (the *multazim*) paid fixed fee to government for right to collect local taxes, usually from peasants, but also applied to urban taxes. It was prevalent in Arab provinces.

Imām 1. "Prayer Leader" of whole community of believers; as such, was a title of caliphs.

2. For Ismāᶜīlī and Ithnā ᶜAsharī Shīᶜī, the Imām, is the necessary, divinely guided, infallible, sinless political/religious leader.

iqṭāᶜ Medieval administrative grant, whereby land revenues but not ownership were turned over to a *muqtaᶜ* in return for service, usually military. This tax-farming system has often been mistranslated as "fief."

ᶜirḍ "Honor," particularly of a family/ lineage. Usually related to virtue of a family's female members.

ᶜirfān "Gnosis." Mystically attained knowledge.

Irgun Irgun Zvai Leumi (national military organization). Founded in 1937 by Palestinian Jews as a military organization, whose goal was to establish a Jewish state by any means, but not necessarily under Jewish Agency control. Nucleus of Herut Party in State of Israel.

Islām — Submission to Allāh and accepting Muḥammad as His prophet. To be a Muslim.

ism — Given name of a Muslim; for example, Muḥammad.

Ismāᶜīlī, Ismailites — Member of Shīᶜite sect who believes an infallible Imamate passed from ᶜAlī to his descendants through a seventh Imām (Ismāᶜīl) and to his descendants. Fāṭimids and Assassins were Ismāᶜīlīs. Also called Seveners.

isnād — "Chain of transmitters," particularly applied to chain of those who passed on the *hadīths* until they were collected. Used to verify validity.

istiḥsān — Act of reaching a personal opinion on a legal question without the strict use of analogy.

istiṣlāh — Act of reaching a legal decision by taking the public welfare into account.

Ithnā ᶜAsharī — Member of Shīᶜite sect who believes there were 12 successive Imāms descended from ᶜAlī, the last of whom disappeared but will one day return. Usually translated as the Twelvers or Imāmīs.

īwān — "Vaulted hall/recessed-like room," usually enclosed on 3 sides with the 4th opening onto a courtyard.

_____

Jāhilīya — "Days of Ignorance." The period of Arab history before Islām.

jāmiᶜ — Usually the major or Friday mosque in a city.

Janissary — "New troops." A corruption of the Turkish *yeni cheri*. Refers to

the Ottoman infantry recruited through the *devshirme*.

jazīra — "Island/peninsula." May refer to Arabian Peninsula, the land in northern Iraq and Syria between the Tigris and Euphrates Rivers, or a province in modern Syria.

jihād — Striving in Allāh's path, commonly translated as a Holy War, whose goal is either the expansion or defense of Islām.

jinn, genie — Creatures created from smokeless flame who can appear in different forms and carry out all types of activities. A *jinn*, unlike angels, is subject to judgment like men.

jizya — "Poll/head tax" leveled on *dhimmis* living in Muslim lands.

jund — "Military troop/military settlement" —later a "district/province," especially in Syria.

_____

Kaᶜba — Name of sacred, cube-shaped building in Mecca. Contains the Black Stone (meteorite) which, along with the building, is regarded as holy. Muslims pray toward the Kaᶜba. It serves as a unifying focus among Muslims.

kadi — See *qāḍī*.

kāfir — Applies to an unbeliever or infidel.

kalām — "Debate" (literally); scholastic theology.

kānūn — See *qānūn*.

kānūnnāme — Collection of *kanuns*.

kapi kular — High Ottoman officials who were theoretically "slaves of the Porte."

Kapudan Pāshā — The admiral of the Ottoman fleet.

kātib — A secretary.

kazi ᶜasker/ qāḍī ᶜaskar — Chief military judge. Important under Mamlūks and Ottomans.

khamsīn — Arabic for 50; term for hot desert winds.

khān	Title implies authority; used in post-Mongol Iran for rulers and local governors, but eventually a polite title for males.	Knesset	Israeli Parliament.
		Koran	See *Qur'ān*.
		Kuds	See *al-Quds*.
khān	Large building for travelers and/or merchandise.	Kūfic	A variety of forms of Arabic script, with an emphasis on straight, vertical and horizontal strokes. One of the earliest scripts.
kharāj	The specific meaning has varied but, as a general rule for the pre-Ottoman period, it referrs to the land tax as opposed to *jizya*.	kul [kullar]	"Man of the Sulṭān." Often translated as "slave."
Khārijī, Kharijites	Minor Muslim sect, usually in political opposition to a Sunnī or Shīᶜite ruler. They believed that equality of all believers applied to those qualified for caliph's office, as well as all other offices. Sect appears as Kharijites.	kunya	Patronymic part of a Muslim name: Abū [father of]. May refer to an actual son or be an honorific title, an attribute or a characteristic. Also Umm [mother of].
khaṭīb	The one who gives the *khuṭba*.	Kurd	Person identified with a linguistic (Kurdish) cultural group whose traditional home has been northern Iraq, S.E. Turkey and N.W. Iran. Most Kurds have been engaged in nomadic occupations and are Sunnī Muslims.
khātūm	Mongol title for empresses and other court women; came to be applied to women generally.		
Khedive	Ancient Persian title acquired in 1866 for a high price by Ismāᶜīl, Governor of Egypt. Held by his family members until 1914, when they took title of *Sulṭān*.	laqab	Honorific part of a Muslim name, many times as a compound ending in al-Din or al-Dawla, such as Ṣalāḥ al-Dīn [Saladin]. Now means "family name."
al-Khulafā', al-Rāshidūn	"The Rightly Guided" caliphs. Term refers to the first 4 caliphs: Abū Bakr, ᶜUmar, ᶜUthmān and ᶜAlī (632-661 C.E.).	levend [pl. levendāt]	"Robber/adventurer/irregular fighter/ sailor/one uprooted from the soil."
khums	A 5th of all profit earned in trade; a charitable tax.	madhhab	Refers to the accepted Sunnī legal school or rite, which today number four: Ḥanafī, Ḥanbalī, Mālikī and Shāfiᶜī.
khuṭba	"Sermon"; given at the Friday noon prayer by a *khaṭīb*. Sermon used to disseminate political information and to give religious instruction. A symbol of political sovereignty of a ruler was to mention that ruler's name in the *khuṭba*.	Madīna, Medina	Specifically Madīnat al-Rasūl [City of the Prophet]. Refers to pre-Islamic, western Arabian oasis community at Yathrib, after Muḥammad moved his new politico-religious community there (622 C.E.).
kibbutz [pl. kibbutzim]	Collective, communal, agricultural settlements established in Palestine and Israel by Jews.	madrasa, medrese	Muslim college, originally a Sunnī school for teaching *sharīᶜa*. Term later applied to most secondary
kibla	See *qibla*.		
al-Kitāb	"The Book"; i.e., the *Qur'ān* [Koran].		

	schools that taught the Islamic sciences.
Maghrib	"West." Term came to mean the general area of Libya, Tunisia, Algeria and Morocco. Al-Maghrib is the Arabic name of Morocco.
mahdī	"The Guided One." Usually refers to one who is divinely guided, a Messiah.
majlis	An "assembly" and, today, a "parliament."
malik	"King." Title held by modern monarchs, but relatively rare in earlier times.
Mālikī	Follower of the Sunnī *madhhab*; named after Mālik Ibn Anas.
Mamlūk	"One possessed." Technically meant "a slave," but came to refer to a white male (usually Turkish) who was a member of an elite cavalry corps. They were manumitted after being trained/instructed in Islām. The height of their power was when they controlled Egypt from 1260 to 1517 C.E.
Mapai	Major Israeli political party, labor and socialist, which has dominated Israeli governments until 1977. Now Ha-ᶜAvoda [Labor] Party.
maqṣūra	Enclosed portion of a mosque where a monarch could pray, separated from the rest of the congregation.
marjaᶜ-i taqlīd	A *mujtahid* whose practices and pronouncements furnish a binding example on those unable to exert independent judgment in matters relating to the religious law.
Maronite	Christian sect, primarily found in Lebanon, that has been in communion with Roman Catholicism since 17th century. Lebanese president is always a Maronite.
mashhad	Tomb of a *shahīd* [martyr].
masjid	A mosque.
mawlā [pl. mawālī]	"Client." Relationship by which a non-kin person could be brought

	into a tribe; one system used to bring non-Arabs into the early Muslim system. Also used to refer to a religious leader: *mawlānā* [our lord], or as a form of address to a ruler, in the sense of "my lord."
Mawlid al-Nabī	Muḥammad's birthday, celebrated on Rabīᶜ I, 12.
medrese	See *madrasa*.
Melchite, Melkite	A sect that broke from Greek Orthodox and is in communion with Roman Catholicism [Greek Catholic].
miḥna	"Court of inquiry/trial," particularly associated with Muᶜtazilite position of some of the early ᶜAbbāsid caliphs.
miḥrāb	"Niche" in the *qibla* wall of a mosque. It signifies the direction of prayer.
millet, milla	An internally autonomous religious community in Ottoman Empire. The 3 major *millet*s were: Armenian Orthodox, Greek Orthodox and Jewish.
manāra/minaret/mi'dana	The tower of a mosque from which the *muezzin* gives the call to prayer.
minbar	The pulpit in a mosque from which the *khuṭba* is given.
mīrī	"Government" or "publicly owned property."
miṣr [pl. amsār]	"Garrison center." Term used for Fustāṭ and, generally, for Egypt.
Monophysite	Member of an Eastern church, who believes Christ has a single nature.
mudīr	"Director" or "administrator."
mu'adhdhin	The one who calls the faithful to prayer 5 times daily: *adhān*.
muezzin	See *mu'adhdhin*.
muftī	Person trained in the *sharīᶜa*, who gives a non-binding legal opinion [*fatwā*] in response to questions submitted to him.

Muhājirūn	Meccan emigrants who joined Muḥammad in Medina.
Muḥarram	First month of Muslim year. On the 10th of the month, Shī^cites mourn the martyrdom of Ḥusayn, ^CAlī's son, at Karbala in 61/680.
muḥtasib	"Market inspector," who was also in charge of enforcing public moral-ity. See also *ḥisba*.
mujtahid	Person who exercised personal inter-pretation of the *sharī^ca* to form a legal opinion. Shī^cites permit their ^c*ulamā'* this role; while, for most periods, it was denied to most Sunnī ^c*ulamā'*. See also *ijtihād*.
mukhtār	"Head of a village" in Greater Syria.
mulk	"Private property."
mullā, mollā	Member of the ^c*ulamā'*, but particu-larly applied to Shī^cite ^c*ulamā'* of Iran. The title is earned when one has reached the 2nd level of Shī^cite education and has master-ed one book of *fiqh*.
mültezim, multazim	The holder of an *iltizam*.
Munāfiqūn	Medinan group who rejected Muḥammad's message; translated as "hypo-crites."
muqarnas	An architectural, decorative element, which are also called "stalactite" or "honeycomb" vaults.
murshid	A "spiritual guide" on the *ṣūfī* path.
Muslim	"One who submits." The official name for those who accept Islām.
Mu^ctazilī	A member of a particular school of Islamic rational thought, strong-ly influenced by Hellenism. The sect is called Mutazilite.

nabī	"A prophet," while al-Nabī or al-Nabī al-Ummī refers to Muḥammad.
nā'ib	A "deputy" or "delegate."
nasab	The part of a Muslim name that re-fers to his/her lineage; i.e., *ibn* or *bint* [son/daughter] of an immediate or distant ancestor.

Naskh	General name for cursive Arabic scripts. Refers to a specific form, which is small and highly legible. One of earliest scripts.
naṣrānī [pl. naṣārā]	A Christian.
Nasta^cliq	This script, invented in 14th cen-tury, is extremely popular in areas influenced by Persian. It has short verticals, sloping hor-izontals, and has been described as "hanging."
Nestorian	Christian sect which holds that Christ has two separate natures: a divine and a human one. Members were found in Iraq/Iran/Syria.
nisba	The adjectival part of a Muslim name, which can denote family origin, profession, etc.
Nuṣayrī	Follower of an extreme Shī^cite group in Syria, who believes ^cAlī is the incarnation of the Deity. See Alawite.

Osmanlı	An Ottoman; i.e., one who was a Mus-lim, knew Ottoman ways; and, or-iginally, in theory, a "slave of the Sulṭān."

padishāh	A Persian title for rulers, used by Ottoman emperors.
Pahlavi	1. Name of a former dynasty ruling Iran until 1979. 2. Name of pre-Islamic form of Mid-dle Persian.
Pāsdārān [plural]	A general Persian name for "guards," applied since 1979 to the Revo-lutionary Guards of the Islamic Republic of Iran.
pāshā, paşa	Turkish title of very high rank, normally military, under the Ottomans. Held by Ottoman offi-cials into the 20th century.
pīr	A title for the head of a *ṣūfī* or-

	der. Also means "elder" or "veteran."
Porte	See Sublime Porte.
qāḍī	Muslim judge learned in the *sharīᶜa*, whose decisions were legally binding.
qānūn	Laws issued by Ottoman *sulṭān*s, based on their right of ᶜ*urf* [custom], as opposed to laws based on the *sharīᶜa*.
qānūnnāme	A collection of *qānūn*s.
qibla	"The direction of prayer." Also refers to the wall of any mosque facing the Kaᶜba in Mecca which has a *miḥrāb*.
qirā'a	Certificate that verifies that a student has read the text aloud before the holder of the *ijāza*. Recitation of the *Qur'ān*.
qiyās	Process of juridical reasoning by analogy that is accepted by Sunnī *madhhab*s as one of the sources of the *sharīᶜa*.
al-Quds	"The Holy Place," in particular the Muslim name for Jerusalem.
al-Qur'ān, Koran	The Muslim Holy Book. Considered divine, contains God's revelations as given in Arabic to Muḥammad, and is the basis for the Islamic way of life.
Quraysh	Name of the major Meccan clan [6th-7th centuries] into which Muḥammad was born. Medieval Muslim political theorists believed that a caliph, to be legitimate, had to be descended from the Quraysh through the male line.
ra'īs, reis	"Chief/leader/president/etc." of a modern state. Sometimes used as part of a compound name. Also "sea captain" or "Ottoman naval commander."
raᶜīya/rayah/	"A flock." In the Ottoman Empire it
reᶜaya	initially meant all non-Osmanlı, but eventually came to refer only to non-Muslim taxpayers.
rakᶜa	One cycle of the prayer ritual, including bowing and prostration.
Ramaḍān	Ninth month of Muslim year, when Muslims are to fast from dawn to sunset.
rasūl	"Messenger," but also used to refer to prophets as "messengers of God."
ra'y	"Personal opinion." Muslim juridical term implying personal speculation.
razzia, ghazwa	A Bedouin raid.
ribāṭ	A *sūfī* hospice; originally a fortified military hospice.
Ridda	"Apostasy." In particular, refers to breaking away from Islām by a number of tribes, just before and immediately following the death of Muḥammad.
risāla [pl. rasā'il]	A treatise.
Rūm	First the Byzantine (Roman) Empire, then Anatolia, particularly under Seljuk rule.
Rumeli	Ottoman territories in Europe.
Sabra	1. A Jew born in Palestine or Israel since the late 19th century A.D. 2. Cactus fruit with prickly exterior and sweet interior.
Ṣadr Aᶜẓam	Ottoman title for the Grand Wazīr.
ṣaḥn	The courtyard of a mosque.
ṣalāt	Prayer 5 times a day. One of the so-called 5 pillars of Islām: *shahādah/zakāt/ṣawm/ḥajj*.
samāᶜ	Certificate stating that a student has attended a reading presided over by one holding an *ijāza*.
sancak, sanjak	Ottoman military or administrative district. The number of *sanjak*s varied in different periods.

sāqiya — Water wheel used for raising water into an irrigation canal/ditch.

saray/serail/ seraglio — "Palace." Later, the "seat of government." For Europeans, the women's quarters of a palace: *harīm.*

sardār — "Military commander." Title was held even by Englishmen when they were Commanders-in-Chief of the Egyptian army.

ṣawm — "Fasting/abstinence." Al-Ṣawm is the legal, prescribed fast during the month of Ramaḍān.

sayyid — "Master/lord/etc.," but became an honorific title for Muḥammad's descendants. Used today for "mister."

Sephardim — Jews whose ancestors came from Spain, knew the Spanish Jewish rites and, possibly, spoke Ladino. Term has sometimes been applied to Mediterranean, Middle Eastern or "Oriental" Jews.

shādūf — Means of raising irrigation water with a counterweight in Egypt.

Shāfiᶜī — Follower of the Sunnī *madhhab,* named after Shāfiᶜī

shāh — "King." Title used by a number of Persian dynasties.

shahāda — Bearing witness to Muslim creed by stating: "There is no God but Allāh, and Muḥammad is His Messenger." One of the 5 duties of a Muslim: *hajj/salāt/ṣawm/zakāt.*

shahīd — A "martyr," a particularly important concept for Shīᶜites.

sharīᶜa — Islamic law based on the *Qur'ān, hadīth, qiyās* and *ijmāᶜ.*

sharīf — A title meaning "highborn/noble." Came to be applied to the descendants of ᶜAlī's son, Ḥasan.

shaykh/şeyh/ sheikh — Literally "old man." Used as a title of respect to refer variously to: head of a tribe/leader of a village/head of a *sūfī* order/head of a Muslim guild.

Shaykh al- Islām, şeyhülislām — Title of leading religious figure, aside from the caliph in a Muslim state. Under the Mamlūks he was a *qāḍī* while, eventually, the Ottomans appointed the *muftī* of Istanbul to the office.

shayṭān — The devil, Satan.

Shīᶜa — That group of Muslims, who split from Islamic community over caliphate issue, believe the caliphate is hereditary and should have gone to ᶜAlī and his descendants. Have further divided into many groups, including the Ithnā ᶜAsharī and Ismāᶜīlīs. Became dominant political force in Iran in 16th C.

Shīᶜī, — Follower of the Shīᶜa; the sect is called Shīᶜite.

shurṭa — Police.

silsilā — For a *sūfī* order, the chain of transmitters of their knowledge.

sipāhī — Cavalryman in the Ottoman Empire, usually holding a *timar.*

sīra — "Biography," but particularly associated with the biography of Muḥammad.

Sublime Porte — European translation of *Bāb-i ᶜAlī* [high gate]. Term stood for the Ottoman Grand Wazīr office and, eventually, Ottoman government.

ṣūfī — Generic term for Muslim "mystic." Derived from Arabic for "wool," referring to a person wearing a wool robe and living an ascetic life. Later meant a member of a *tarīqa* or *sūfī* order.

sulṭān — Title that came to mean "supreme secular power." Primarily associated with rulers of Turkish origin.

sunna — Customary procedure for living that came to mean "the way and customs of Muḥammad and his companions."

Sunnī — "One who follows the way of Muḥammad," particularly those who accept one

	of the 4 *madhhab*s, as opposed to Shī^cī sects. Sometimes mistranslated as "orthodox." The majority sect among Muslims.
sūq	Marketplace.
sūra	A chapter in the *Qur'ān*.
tafsīr	Qur'ānic exergesis.
takbīr	The phrase *Allāhu akbar* [God is great].
Tanzimat	"Reordering/reorganization." Term used to describe period of modernization and Westernization in the Ottoman Empire (mid-19th century).
taqīya	Act by which a person disavows his true beliefs when such avowal would threaten his well-being. Practiced by Ismā^cīlīs and other Shī^cī sects at various times.
taqlīd	"Imitation," in the sense of blind acceptance and following of the *sharī^ca*, as expounded in the various *madhhab*s.
ta'rīkh	"Era/dating." It became the general name for "history/a chronicle/ annals."
ṭarīqa	Term applied to *ṣūfī* orders, as well as the path followed by them to reach gnosis.
ta^czīya	The commemoration in dramatic performances of the martyrdom of the Imāms, particularly that of Imām Ḥusayn at Karbala.
tekke	Building in which *ṣūfī* members of an order live and perform rituals.
Thuluth	A large, cursive script. The verticals have a leftward slant, while the horizontals have a deep curve.
timar	Ottoman grant of income from a tax source, usually land, in return for services—in particular, for the Ottoman cavalry: *sipāhī*s.
timarcı, timariot	The holder of a *timar*.

ṭirāz	State factories that produce fine cloth. Term became associated with the inscribed bands on the cloths, and even inscribed bands on buildings.
Tūdeh	A Leftist; then meant the Communist Party of Iran.
tugh	Ottoman badge of rank (crest or pennant of horse tails) attached to a flagstaff.
tughra	Official signature of Ottoman *sulṭān*s.
turjumān	"Translator/interpreter." See *dragoman*.
turkman, turkoman	A Turkic-speaking nomad.
^culamā', ulema [s. ^cālim]	Refers to those learned in Islām. Sometimes translated as the "Muslim clergy."
^cumda	"Head/chief" of a village, particularly used in Egypt.
'umma	The "community" of Islamic faithful. Also used in modern sense of a "nation" or "people."
^curf	"Custom/customary practice," having a limited/restricted role as a *sharī^ca* source, but used extensively by Ottomans. See *qānūn*.
usūl al-fiqh	Four sources or "roots of law": *Qur'ān*, *ḥadīth*, *ijmā^c* and *qiyās*.
ūsulīs	The dominant Ithnā ^cAsharī Shī^cite legal tradition, which emphasizes the use of reason within the confines of religion.
vali, wālī	"Governor," particularly of a *vilayet*.
vilayet, wilāya	An Ottoman administrative unit of varying size and number.
wādī	A "valley/river/dry river bed."
wafd	"Delegation." Name of the major Egyptian political party founded by Sa^cd Zaghlūl.

wakil, vakil	"Representative/deputy."
waqf	Prior endowment, whereby revenues from a particular source are permanently allocated for purposes of public benefit, such as the building of a mosque.
wazīr/vezir/ vizier	Advisor to a ruler who, under the early ᶜAbbāsids and other dynasties, was the equivalent of a Prime Minister.
wuḏū	Ritual ablutions.
yishuv	Name for the Jewish community in Palestine before 1948.
yörük, yürük	Nomads in Turkey. Turkish nomads in the Balkans.
zakāt	Obligatory alms tax on all Muslims.
zeamet, ziᶜamet	Ottoman *timar*, with an annual revenue between 20,000 and 100,000 *aqçe*.
zimmī	See *ahl al-Dhimma*.

Historical Atlas Index

** Diacritical marks have been omitted.

148

**Diacritical marks have been omitted.

152